Pigza, Jessica

.........................................................................

BiblioCraft

.........................................................................


.........................................................................

explore and discover

collect and learn

wonder and reveal

# BIBLIO *Craft*

A Modern Crafter's Guide to Using Library Resources
to Jumpstart Creative Projects

## JESSICA PIGZA

PHOTOGRAPHS BY JOHNNY MILLER

PHOTOSTYLING BY SHANA FAUST     ILLUSTRATIONS BY SUN YOUNG PARK

stc craft / a melanie falick book

NEW YORK

# contents

# FOREWORD

*Dear Reader,*

Libraries at almost any scale are places of inspiration, providing information and entertainment as well as the opportunity to pursue education, self-improvement, creative quests, and new knowledge. The New York Public Library, with its vast collections and the beautiful architecture of its main building, is particularly inspirational. However, the talent, dedication, and expertise of the staff are what excite me most about the Library.

Jessica Pigza is a wonderful example. Her creativity, her passion, and her "love of the hunt" for information and ideas make her an excellent reference practitioner, and her particular joy in helping others become energized by something they find in the Library is why she wrote this book. In the following pages, Jessica leads readers on a tour of different types of libraries, collections, and other resources that can supply design ideas and motivation for all sorts of curious and creative souls. She also provides a practical guide for examining the contents of the best digital libraries and imparts important tips on the application of library materials beyond personal use.

For both the apprehensive and the eager, this guide to libraries, books, ephemera, and more is as approachable as the librarian behind it. There is plenty of guidance on these pages for learning about new resources and for trying something new. And it is full of projects that illustrate the artistic, imaginative creations that can result when you turn to libraries for discovery. From home goods such as Natalie Chanin's cyanotype-inspired throw and Grace Bonney's natural history votive candles to embellishments like Rebecca Ringquist's cartouche embroidery and Julie Schneider's wood type–patterned stationery, each project began with an encounter with unique and unexpected library materials. I am delighted by the existence of this wonderful book because of the innovative uses of libraries and collections it is sure to spark. I won't keep you any further from being inspired. See you at the library!

Ann Thornton

ANDREW W. MELLON DIRECTOR
THE NEW YORK PUBLIC LIBRARY

# INTRODUCTION

*I'm lucky to work as a rare book librarian* at the New York Public Library, one of the nation's largest research libraries, with unparalleled collections of both antiquarian and new books, handwritten documents, maps, vast runs of magazines, and more. On any given day, I might assist a graphic designer who is interested in finding examples of a particular early typeface, or help a children's book specialist to compare illustrations used in different editions of an iconic children's story. I might assist in identifying a previous owner of a volume in the library's collection, based on the bookplate found within the book. Or I might welcome a class of history students from a local college who have come to learn how early printed books were printed, folded, and bound by hand. A big part of what I love about being a rare book librarian is the chance to learn about and discuss the artisanal skills needed to make books during the handpress era. From how paper was made to what sewing stitches were used for bindings to historical ink recipes, I'm always curious to learn more.

While I didn't necessarily appreciate early printed books when I was a kid growing up in a small town in western Pennsylvania, I did grow up immersed in a world of crafts of all kinds. My mother made clothes for me and my sister, and my mother's own mother worked in a fabric shop and was a skilled seamstress (among many other things, she made fabulous clothes for my Barbie doll, including a leopard fur cape that I still have). At home I had plenty of chances to dabble in all sorts of crafts, including macramé, ceramics, candle-wicking, punched tin, crochet, plastic canvas, cross-stitch, and even cornhusk doll–making. And I'm forever grateful that my mother taught me how to use her sewing machine, because I've been making my own dresses and skirts for years.

My love for making things by hand has long been tied to books. As a kid I loved poring over pattern catalogs when my mother took my sister and me to the fabric store.

School texts from one hundred years ago can reveal how students learned to measure, draw, and stitch in the past, and they led Brett Bara to create geometry-inspired fabric pyramids (page 170).

And my recollections of paging though my mother's craft books have led me to try to add vintage titles like *The Woman's Day Book of Soft Toys and Dolls* (1975) and *The Good Housekeeping New Complete Book of Needlecraft* (1971) to my own library at home. In some cases I've succeeded in persuading her to give me her copies, and in others I've tracked down and purchased copies for myself. This way, I can remake a favorite afghan or a beloved stuffed hippo whenever I'm ready.

I've always loved poking around at flea markets and used book shops for interesting old arts and crafts publications. Strangely, however, it wasn't until I had been working at the New York Public Library for a few months that it dawned on me that I was basically sitting on top of a craft book gold mine. The fateful day arrived when I was invited to start blogging for the library on whatever topic interested me, and my colleague Rebecca Federman pointed out the obvious—that I should write about crafts. From that day forward, I've wandered through the stacks, I've dug around in our catalog, and I've found vintage patterns, 1920s needlework magazines, Victorian home decorating guides, 1970s DIY books for kids, nineteenth-century type specimen books, and other unique sources of inspiration to share with the curious.

Always eager to spread news of my library's collection further, I've gone beyond blog posts and have also offered small instructional classes to the public, during which I help people learn how to use the library to find their own vintage craft inspiration. I've also been hosting Handmade Crafternoons at the library since 2009, with the help

Type specimen books like this 1872 example from William H. Page & Co. offer eye candy for typophiles. Julie Schneider studied books like this when designing her stationery (page 82).

of my cohost and library volunteer Maura Madden. Each of these free events is built around a theme and includes a special guest, a project, and a spread of books from the library's collections. These events draw in a variety of people who all share an interest in handicraft and handmade material culture, and it's been heartwarming and emboldening to see a community like this form at my library. Especially memorable events in this series have included weaving on DIY looms, making personalized radial maps, and creating handmade pop-up books.

My outreach efforts have taken a few surprising turns as well. At a local yarn shop, I had a fabulous time giving a talk on finding vintage knitting and crochet patterns in the library. I've also had fun sharing selected items from the library's collection with designer and illustrator Heather Ross's workshop students (a hands-down favorite book with the group was an eighteenth-century natural history of fish with unbelievably colored, practically kaleidoscopic illustrations). I was even fortunate enough to work on a video series in collaboration with Design*Sponge, called Design by the Book, in which I matched five wonderful artists with library collections that inspired them to create new work. Each artist gave me a wish list of research topics, and it was just as exciting for me to discover sources in the library that were new to me—including illustrated histories of wrought iron, fanciful books on space travel, and fabric swatch catalogs—as it was to observe how each artist transformed what he or she saw at the library into a new creation. The artist and illustrator Julia Rothman, for example, created a repeating

Pictured above are just a few designs among ten thousand included in a 1915 guide to Japanese heraldry that Molly Schnick examined when creating her felt coasters (page 164).

pattern of men in uniform inspired by a pictorial directory of military insignia, and she used her design on a limited-edition pillow she named, appropriately, At Ease.

All of these outreach efforts left me in awe of the potential for design inspiration in the unique collections of research libraries. But I wanted to spread the excitement further. Recognizing that a lot of people are intimidated by the library or uncertain about how to use one to delve deeply into a subject that interests them, I decided to write this book. In Part One of *BiblioCraft*, you can brush up on your library skills, from call numbers to catalog searches. You'll also find a go-to guide to the ins and outs of different kinds of libraries, tips for making the most of a visit to the library, and even some comforting advice on copyright. In addition, I include suggestions for dozens of libraries, digital collections, other specialized sources in a variety of topics—from type design to children's books, home economics to the cartographic arts—that can jumpstart your own library explorations. All of these tips will help you build your skills so you can start hunting for inspiration of all kinds. It will also give you a strong starting point for initiating conversations with librarians. All the librarians I know love to connect readers with the materials they need, so don't be shy about asking us for help. We are there for you—in person or via chat, e-mail, or phone—so talk to us about what kinds of sources you'd like to find.

Part Two: Projects Inspired by the Library is where you get to see library inspiration in action in 22 projects. To illustrate the potential of library collections, I invited fifteen talented makers to join me in designing projects inspired by library collections.

Gretchen Hirsch's study of hats and hairstyles led her to *British Millinery* (March 1950 issue above left, with her rose fascinator [page 140]) and *Godey's Lady's Book* (1849 illustration above right).

Heraldry manuals became coasters, soil charts led to a children's growth chart, and a botanical work inspired a hand-stenciled and -stitched throw. The stuff of antiquarian books—marbled papers, decorated bookbindings, and historical watermarks—resulted in a colorful zipper pouch, a quilled pendant, and embroidered pillows. The lure of letterforms, both printed and handwritten, inspired unique snowflakes, stamped cards, a pegboard cross-stitch, and a redwork bird.

Assisting my contributors offered me the same fun and challenges I face when helping any library user make the most of the library's collections, but with the added excitement that I was helping people who have been inspiring me with their work for years, and that I'd get to witness the entire process, from their library studies to a finished project (that I'd get to feature in my book). Sometimes I worried that I overwhelmed a contributor with too much information. Molly Schnick, for instance, was immediately taken with the graphic possibilities inherent in Japanese heraldry designs and knew right away that she wanted to create coasters. But the hard part came in choosing which designs to transform, when she was sitting with thousands and thousands of design options before her eyes. When Gretchen Hirsch visited my library to study the vintage millinery magazines and books we'd identified as being right for her research, her eyes widened at the sight of an entire rolling cart of materials set aside for her. She ended up making multiple visits to the library because she didn't want to miss any possible inspiration, and her resulting fascinator highlights the glamour of the pages she studied.

In Joseph LeConte's *Elements of Geology,* varied textural patterns designate different rock and soil layers, and these striping diagrams inspired Liesl Gibson when designing her soil profile growth chart (page 132).

Another worry was that one of my contributors would want something I couldn't uncover in the library. Liesl Gibson was interested in historical graphic depictions of soil profiles and geological formations. My response was something like, "Hmm, well, yes, I'm sure we have these." But I spend most of my time with history, literature, and art, not science, so I didn't have any ideas to start with. I did what I always do whenever a reader asks for help with an unfamiliar topic—I did a bit of research myself to get up to speed, I identified a few key Subject Headings to search, and I made sure I found illustrated books on the topic for her to examine. And her resulting growth chart was a thrill to see.

Whenever I worry about finding what a reader needs, I always remind myself that being a librarian isn't about knowing the answers; it's about the fun of knowing how to find the answers. When it came to working with each talented contributor, though, the most exciting part was getting to see the unexpected directions that some projects took. Julie Schneider's projects use wood type designs in ways I'd not have imagined—as a repeating pattern on a stamp, and as a hidden element in a cut paper snowflake. Anna Bondoc's bookplate, while inspired by the Arts and Crafts movement, remains thoroughly modern and bright. And Natalie Chanin's use of contemporary poetry adds a textual richness to her throw that, while unexpected when she chose to add it, seems integral now.

Working with each designer revealed surprises, too, all of which have since convinced me that I got started on *BiblioCraft* at exactly the right moment. For example, I learned that Mary Corbet had been thinking about turning ornamental penmanship into

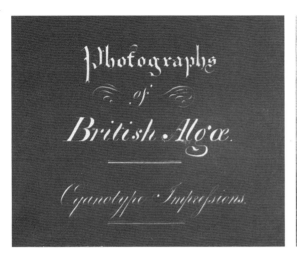

Botanist Anna Atkins used the cyanotype process to create *Photographs of British Algae* in 1843. Nearly two hundred years later, Natalie Chanin studied Atkins's images when creating her throw (page 118).

embroidery for a while before I approached her to ask if she'd want to try something along those lines. Haley Pierson-Cox knew her way around the world of digitized rare books from a previous job, and had long admired hand-lettering found in illuminated manuscripts and other hand-lettered works. Rebecca Ringquist is a regular visitor to my library, and shortly before I wrote to introduce myself and invite her to participate in my book project, she learned about me through the Design by the Book videos and wondered if she could ask me about using the library's special collections for her work.

Serendipity plays a part in any research. One book leads to another, a historical illustration in a modern book leads to more art by that illustrator, or a chance conversation with a librarian leads to a collection that's perfect for a design project. By allowing serendipity to play alongside some basic library skills, you can find the inspiration you seek in libraries of all kinds. Whether you think of a library as a stately building downtown, a humble little haven tucked into your small neighborhood, or a digital collection open all night online, it's easier and more satisfying than ever to make the most of what libraries have to offer. I hope that with *BiblioCraft* in hand you'll feel excited and ready to explore, discover, and create.

PART ONE

# FINDING INSPIRATION AT THE LIBRARY

Whether you 're looking for a quiet spot to read or a humming atmosphere among other seekers, a library reading room might offer just the environment you seek. At some libraries, the architectural details themselves can even offer inspiration. The decorative elements shown here—all part of the New York Public Library's historic Stephen A. Schwarzman Building—might lead you to create Beaux Arts-inspired stencils, repeating patterns, paper cuts, or other original designs. As you explore *BiblioCraft*, you'll see occasional glimpses of this landmark building and its books and collections (like those on the rolling cart at left), since the photographs were taken at this library.

# LIBRARY COLLECTIONS

*Do you need the newest issue of a home design magazine,* or one from a hundred years ago? Are you on the hunt for vintage maps, or is it historical handwriting samples that you seek? Do you want to attend a craft social, or meet a children's book illustrator? Different kinds of libraries offer different kinds of materials, services, and programs. And when you're on the hunt for design inspiration, you'll find library collections near, far, and at your fingertips, too. From your local neighborhood libraries offering the newest craft books and stitching circles to internationally known research centers that are home to rare early editions, the right library for your next creative project is waiting to give you the inspiration you need.

## BRANCH LIBRARIES IN YOUR NEIGHBORHOOD

The libraries you are probably most familiar with are those in your own neighborhoods. These are often called branch libraries because they are part of a network of similar neighborhood libraries spread across a town or region. Each branch library focuses its offerings—books, magazines, and events—on what those who live nearby need and want.

Branch libraries work hard to strengthen community connections through programs, and your local branch might offer knitting nights, sewing circles, and other arts and crafts events for adults, children, and families. Through these events you can make new connections, share ideas with fellow enthusiasts, and dedicate a few hours to fostering your creativity by working on your own projects or exploring the books around you. If your branch library doesn't offer any crafting nights and you think there's an audience, ask your librarian about adding one to their calendar to give it a try. A "bring-your-own-craft" night is an easy option to start with, because it requires just a meeting space for attendees who bring along their own works-in-progress.

Branch libraries are set up to encourage browsing, with open shelves of materials organized according to subject categories. And when you've found just the right sources, you can use your library card to borrow them and take them home.

A branch library usually offers selections of recent books and magazines on craft, literature, history, and art. Because these libraries have very limited space to shelve and display collections for browsing, branch libraries don't tend to keep older materials that have fallen out of high demand. When it comes to periodicals—magazines, journals, and newspapers—a branch library will often have the most recent issues of these at hand but won't often have decades-old issues on the shelf.

Your local branch library may, however, be able to access many resources beyond its own walls, if it belongs to a network of related libraries that shares collections. If you need a source that's held in a different library, ask a librarian at your local branch if she or he can help you to borrow it through an interlibrary loan program.

## RESEARCH LIBRARIES

What if you want to look through cookbooks from a century ago, or see what knitting books in the nineteenth century looked like, or read millinery magazines from the 1940s? In these cases, it's a research library that you need, because that's where you'll find older books and magazines, unique collections, and rare materials. Although some research libraries are not open to the public, many are, so if a library intrigues you, find out about the possibility of visiting. (See Planning Your Library Visit on page 28 for more tips).

Research libraries may be part of a university. For example, when embroidery artist Mary Corbet began her research into ornamental penmanship designs, she worked with digitized portions of the Zaner-Bloser Penmanship Collection held at the Weinberg Memorial Library at the University of Scranton (Scranton, Pennsylvania). My own interest in turning the geometric patterns of early hand-drawn nautical maps called portolan charts into stitched wall art led me to the digital collections of Yale University's Beinecke Rare Book and Manuscript Library in New Haven, Connecticut.

Research libraries are often tied to museums, historical societies, or other organizations. The Metropolitan Museum of Art, for example, boasts a dozen different libraries and study centers in New York City, including the Thomas J. Watson Library, which is its central research center, as well as the Antonio Ratti Textile Center and Reference Library. And the American Antiquarian Society, based in Worcester, Massachusetts, is a scholarly center with a major research collection devoted to early Americana, including type specimen books like those artist Julie Schneider turned to in her search for paper cut inspiration.

Some research libraries are associated with federal or state governments or agencies. The Library of Congress (www.loc.gov) is the nation's largest and most complex government-associated research library. Located in Washington, DC, it's

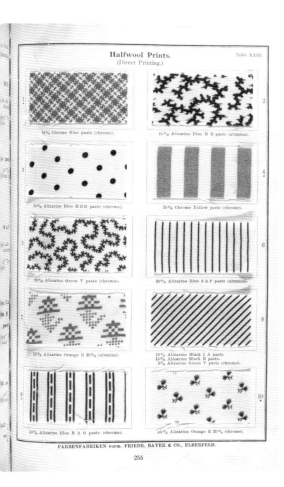

Halfwool Prints.
(Direct Printing.)

Table XXIII.

1. 15% Chrome Blue paste (chrome).
2. 15% Alizarine Blue H R paste (alumina).
3. 15% Alizarine Blue H B B paste (chrome).
4. 15% Chrome Yellow paste (chrome).
5. 20% Alizarine Green V paste (chrome).
6. 20% Alizarine Blue S A P paste (alumina).
7. 15% Alizarine Orange R 20% (alumina).
8. 15% Alizarine Black I A paste. 15% Alizarine Black B paste. 5% Alizarine Green V paste (chrome).
9. 10% Alizarine Blue B A G paste (chrome).
10. 45% Alizarine Orange R 20% (chrome).

FARBENFABRIKEN vorm. FRIEDR. BAYER & CO., ELBERFELD.

255

PETERSON'S MAGAZINE, MAY, 1862.

KNITTED SHAWL.

If you'd like to immerse yourself in the design history of a particular period or uncover vintage handicraft patterns, research libraries can help. CLOCKWISE FROM ABOVE: Peterson's Magazine offered nineteenth-century American women knitting patterns, including this shawl in 1862. This page from *Combinaisons Ornementales se Multipliant à l'Infini à l'Aide du Miroir* reveals the visual riches within original art nouveau design studies. The August 1867 issue of Godey's Lady's Book presented an adaptable design for a deer; this could be used for cross-stitch, mosaics, and more. Textile industry publications like this 1902 volume entitled The Mordant Dyestuffs of the *Farbenfabriken vorm* often include fabric swatches.

STAG'S HEAD, TO BE WORKED IN ZEPHYR.
The required colors are seven shades of brown, two of gray, and three of green.

*Explanation of Characters.*—■ very deep brown; ▨ a shade lighter; ▨ a shade lighter; ▨ lighter still, and of a yellow shade; ▨ quite a light shade of brown; ▨ a still lighter shade of brown; ▌a shade of brown so light that it is almost white; ✗ dark gray; ▨ a lighter shade of gray; □ dark green; ▨ a medium shade of green; ▨ a light shade of green.

also the largest library in the world. It opens its doors to researchers worldwide in its mission to "support the Congress in fulfilling its constitutional duties and to further the progress of knowledge and creativity for the benefit of the American people." It is home to the nation's Copyright Office, which means that it accepts thousands of newly published materials every day, adding to its astounding historical collection. The Library of Congress also offers a robust and ever-growing selection of well-organized sources online, from programs that include the American Folklife Center, which documents vernacular art, folklore, and handmade material culture, and the American Memory Project, which provides free and open access to the publications, archives, and art that document American history and creativity. There are many smaller libraries tied to the government, however, and some contributors to this book used their materials. Digitized holdings of the U.S. National Library of Medicine (Bethesda, Maryland), for example, provided writer Grace Bonney with Conrad Gessner's sixteenth-century animal illustrations for her votive holders.

Other countries also have their own government-sponsored libraries. In London, the British Library (www.bl.uk) is a giant research library with collections rooted in the eighteenth-century founding of the British Museum and its unprecedented holdings of early printed books. Their online offerings continue to grow, with digitized books and online exhibitions highlighting their most visually engaging collections as well as a Historic Bindings Database with photographs of early handmade bindings (which quilling artist Ann Martin used when she designed her pendant). And they support working artists and designers with courses in entrepreneurship as well as programs that encourage the creative use of their collections.

There are research libraries tied to big U.S. cities as well. Often these institutions are hybrids of a sort, offering neighborhood coverage with a system of branch libraries while also maintaining unique research collections. From Boston to Seattle, Chicago to New York, and San Francisco to Philadelphia (just to name a few), city libraries might surprise you. At the New York Public Library in New York City (www.nypl.org), the research collections are divided broadly by topic into four separate research libraries: the New York Public Library for the Performing Arts; the Schomburg Center for Research in Black Culture; the Science, Industry, and Business Library; and the Stephen A. Schwarzman Building with its focus on humanities and social sciences. Many of the projects within this book were inspired by materials found within the research collections of the New York Public Library. There are magazines, sheet music, picture collections, historical children's books, moving images, manuscripts, and more, spanning centuries, held among these locations. Online sources continue to multiply, with digital images, online exhibitions, and other multimedia programs that highlight the collections. If you live in or near a city, get to know your city's library; you might be happy at the unexpected inspiration available there.

Regardless of what organization, institution, or agency is behind them, all of these research libraries collect with both the immediate needs of their users as well as future potential research questions in mind. They also often work to acquire books and magazines that cover subjects over long periods of time, which leads to collections with historical depth as well as broad coverage. For a creative person in search of inspiration, this means that research libraries can be inspirational gold mines.

Research libraries may have systems and rules that can be confounding to a new user, however. For example, some store part or all of their collection in closed stacks, which means you can't browse for books on your own. You might not be permitted to check books out, and you might need to request access in advance. But the fun of paging through century-old arts textbooks, early printed architectural elevations, or millinery industry publications makes it well worth getting to know how your chosen research library works so you can make the most of its treasures in your creative research.

If you're planning to visit a research library—especially if it's not local to you— it's essential to plan ahead, reach out to the library, and find out as much as possible in advance of your trip. For tips on doing so, see Planning Your Library Visit on page 28.

## SPECIAL COLLECTIONS

A sixteenth-century introduction to all the world's animals, filled with hand-colored woodcut illustrations. A scrapbook full of examples of ornamental penmanship, compiled in the nineteenth century by a teacher of the art. The first photographic work by a woman, who used this newly invented process to document her botanical studies. These are just a few of the items that inspired projects in this book, and each is an example of the kind of rare and special materials held in what are known as "special collections" in research libraries. Such materials are indeed special, and when it comes to design inspiration, these materials hold plenty of visual potential.

What else might you find in a special collection? Historical maps, either hand-drawn, like the portolan chart that inspired my stitched wall hanging, or engraved, like those artist Rebecca Ringquist studied when designing her cartouche, are also often found in special collections. And special collections are usually the place where libraries keep their rarest early printed books, their illuminated manuscripts, and other historical examples of handmade and hand-decorated papers (like the marbled paper that Jodi Kahn used on her zippered pouch).

This illustration feels bold and modern with its graphic presentation of information and its rich color choices, but it is from a book printed in 1908 in Japan.

What is kept in any given special collection depends on the particular library and its subject focus, but generally special collections include early prints, handpress-era books, handwritten documents, and other one-of-a-kind or fragile historical materials. Large research libraries might have different special collections for different kinds of materials—for example, a manuscripts collection, a rare books collection, a photography collection—while smaller libraries often keep all these special materials together in a single special collections area.

There's also the possibility that a library might hold quirky items such as printed ephemera in its special collections. Printed ephemera is just what it sounds like—printed materials that were meant to be used and disposed of; in other words, they were meant to be ephemeral. If you think about the bits of printed matter that you encounter every day—receipts, business cards, train tickets, menus, price tags, play programs, and greeting cards—you'll know that printed ephemera is alive and well today. Now, imagine being able to look at materials like this from decades or centuries ago. Advertising cards, menus, and other older printed ephemera have found their way into special collections, and libraries that own them have started sharing images of them online. One of my favorite of the quirkier special collections in the New York Public Library that you can view online are its cigarette cards. Smaller than baseball cards today, these colorfully illustrated cards came tucked inside cigarette packs and were produced in series on any imaginable topic, from exotic birds to famous battles to cacti (all browsable at digitalgallery.nypl.org).

Because security and conservation are concerns for librarians when they're sharing special collections, these materials are usually made available in a limited-access reading room. Materials may be placed on special desktop cradles or other book support structures to protect the volumes' bindings, and you will likely receive some guidance on how to handle the materials gently. Library staff will monitor the reading room closely, and when you leave, you may be asked to submit your personal belongings to staff for inspection. All of these careful measures make using special collections a little more complicated, but they all serve to protect the materials from thefts, accidents, or mishandling that could jeopardize the future usefulness of these unique works. The good news, though, if you love to uncover inspiration within the kind of stuff held in special collections, is that more and more unique materials are being made available in digitized versions, for easier access. And this means that as a creative maker, you can collect more sources and stories than ever before, whether you visit a special collection in person or online, gathering ideas to use in your own modern designs.

If you plan to make use of a library's special collections, it's important to reach out to the institution, and find out as much as possible in advance of your trip. For tips on doing so, see Planning Your Library Visit on page 28.

# LIBRARY FOR YOU

*Just getting started and wondering which library* might be the right one for you? If you'd like to start exploring locally, see what you can learn about nearby university library collections on their websites. Look into your local public library system as well, because often these libraries have surprising local history collections or other interesting research materials. And while you're at it, ask your local branch librarian for any tips she might have about local libraries in the area. Don't forget to consider museums or historical societies, because these institutions often have library collections as well. Additionally, try searching online for the word "library" and your ZIP code or town name, and see what you find.

There are also, of course, reference books and sites that can guide you to more information about libraries near and far and what their collections contain. Here are a few useful online sources, followed by several print directories. If you'd like to use one of the print directories, ask your local library if they have them among their reference sources.

**Public Libraries.com**    www.publiclibraries.com
This online directory includes listings and links to public libraries, university libraries, state libraries and archives, and even presidential libraries.

**National Libraries.org**    www.nationallibraries.org
National libraries work to collect and document their country's print culture, history, and creative output. This online directory will help you to find out if there's one in your favorite country, so you can see if its collections might suit your creative needs.

**Directory of Digital Collections and Content in Libraries and Museums**
http://imlsdcc.grainger.illinois.edu
This directory lets you discover digital library projects around the country that received support from the Institute of Museum and Library Services.

**Library As Incubator Project**    www.libraryasincubatorproject.org
Founded by three University of Wisconsin–trained librarians, this site reports on digital
and on-site library collections, creative programs, and artist collaborations at libraries
both large and small, all over the world.

**Repositories of Primary Sources**
www.uiweb.uidaho.edu/special-collections/Other.Repositories.html
Created and maintained by scholar Terry Abraham, this is an online directory of
thousands of institutions with holdings of manuscripts, archives, rare books, historical
photographs, and other sources. The primary organizing principle is by location.

*World Guide to Libraries*
München, New York: K. G. Sauer [etc.], 1974–present.
In this regularly updated print directory, more than 40,000 libraries from more than
200 countries are listed. Each entry includes contact information as well as profiles of
holdings and special collections. It is organized by the English form of the country name.
The libraries within include both small and large institutions, from national libraries to
smaller private corporate libraries and archives.

*World Guide to Special Libraries*
München, New York: K. G. Sauer [etc.], 1983–present.
This directory focuses on special libraries, which it defines as those with "thematically
specialized holdings," and its scope includes national libraries as well as various
research libraries. This is organized by subject, and then by country within each subject.
So, for example, in the eighth edition there are sixteen libraries in eight countries listed
as having specialized holdings under the heading Costume, and 122 libraries in thirty
countries under the heading Applied Arts, Industrial Arts, Crafts.

*Subject Collections: A Guide to Special Book Collections and Subject Emphases as
Reported by University, College, Public, and Special Libraries and Museums in the
United States and Canada*
Compiled by Lee Ash and William G. Miller, with the collaboration of Barry Scott, Kathleen
Vickery, and Beverly McDonough. New Providence, New Jersey: R.R. Bowker Co., 1993.
This excellent starting place to learn about the unique, rare, and historic materials held
by libraries in the United States and Canada is organized by subject and geographical
area. It may be an older reference, but it remains a useful way to discover a library
collection you never knew about—maybe one in your own state.

# LIBRARY VISIT

*Once you've found something in a library* that you want to study in person, your next step is to visit the library's website and begin to plan your visit. The more prepared you are, the more effectively you'll be able to spend your time upon arrival. This is especially important if you plan to make use of special collections, since there may be additional steps to take before beginning your work with these rare materials. The following FAQs will help you get started.

### HOW DO I CONTACT THE LIBRARY?

Most libraries have e-mail addresses for sending questions, or chat services. Don't hesitate to contact them.

### IS THE GENERAL PUBLIC PERMITTED TO USE THE LIBRARY?

Some libraries are open to the general public, but others (those that are part of a university) might or might not restrict their visitors to just their own students and faculty. The library's website should explain its admissions policy, but if it doesn't, you can always call and ask.

### DO I NEED A LIBRARY CARD OR ANOTHER KIND OF IDENTIFICATION?

At some libraries you may need to register and get a library card, or at least present a form of identification. Find out, and be sure to bring the proper documents with you.

### DOES THE LIBRARY OFFER RESEARCH ORIENTATION SESSIONS?

Some libraries provide tours or classes to help you to do research at their institution; others offer online guidelines.

### DO I NEED TO COMPLETE A SPECIAL REGISTRATION?

For some collections, a special registration in addition to a library card might be required. You may be asked to provide further details about your research project and the materials you wish to consult.

### ARE THERE FEES?

Libraries may charge admission fees to visitors, and there may be costs associated with some services, such as obtaining photographs or scans.

### DO I NEED AN APPOINTMENT OR CAN I WALK IN?

The answer to this question may depend on what exactly you want to use at that library and when you plan to visit.

### WHERE ARE THE MATERIALS I WANT TO SEE LOCATED? AND WHAT ARE THE HOURS AT THAT LOCATION?

Some libraries have multiple locations, and you want to make sure that you visit the right place at the right day and time.

### DO I NEED TO ORDER MATERIALS IN ADVANCE?

Some libraries store certain materials at off-site locations, and in these cases you might need to order books a day or more in advance of your planned visit so that they can be retrieved and brought out of storage for you.

### CAN I USE A CAMERA, SCANNER, OR COPIER TO CAPTURE IMAGES OF BOOK PAGES FOR LATER REFERENCE?

Many libraries are welcoming and open to library users making their own reproductions, while some remain restrictive, so if you have your heart set on taking photos or scans of book pages, ask in advance if that is permitted. And if it is not, ask if options exist for ordering reproductions to be sent to you.

### CAN I CHECK OUT BOOKS AND TAKE THEM HOME?

In libraries with rare materials and special collections, the answer will likely be no. But newer books might circulate.

### WHAT CAN I BRING WITH ME TO THE LIBRARY WHILE I WORK?

Most libraries have policies about where in the library food and drink are permitted. If you plan to make use of special collections, however, be prepared for greater security as well as limits on what you can bring with you. You can expect not to be able to bring any food, water bottles or other liquids, pens and inks, coats, umbrellas, large totes, or purses into the secure rooms where special collection materials are served. These institutions will provide lockers or coat checks for your belongings, and some institutions will also offer a clear plastic bag for carrying your personal items (like your wallet, phone, pencils, and notepaper) through the library.

Remember, even if things seem overwhelming on your first visit, it's worth the effort to find out how the library you want to use works because the benefits—to your design projects, to access to new inspiration and information, and to feeding your curiosity— are countless. An unfamiliar library and its mysterious processes and policies can seem daunting even to librarians like me who visit libraries in other cities for fun. But once you've learned how things work, how to get what you need for your research project, and where to go for answers when you have questions about the place, you'll feel at home. And, while every library is a little different, once you get a general feel for how a few function, you'll begin to see similarities in policies and systems that will allow you to feel more comfortable each time you enter a new one.

# AT THE LIBRARY

*Even if you haven't visited a library in person lately,* you probably remember the basics—that each book is described in a catalog that you use to find books you want to read, and that each book is assigned a call number that tells you where it can be found on the shelf in the library. By building on this foundation, you'll be ready to start exploring—and exploiting—just about any library that interests you. And while I focus mostly on research libraries, with their unique collections, one-of-a-kind resources, and vivid visual inspiration, the following guide to finding what you want at the library can apply to all libraries generally.

Remember that librarians spend more time than anyone else searching and navigating collections and catalogs, so you should never hesitate to reach out to us. (And who knows, perhaps you'll meet a librarian who wants to collaborate with you—that's what happened when artist and illustrator Heather Ross and I started talking about having her design workshop students take a field trip to my library so that I could share some inspiring sources.) Want to find out if a particular library's famous collection of historic knitting books has been digitized? Need to learn more about the history of mapmaking and wonder what books might help? Ask a librarian! Librarians thrive on finding answers, and most library websites have a place where you can initiate a chat session, send an e-mail, or look up a phone number. Or find one in the flesh if you've already arrived at your favorite research library and have a question about how the place works. While you're talking with a librarian, ask if there are any free orientation classes or tours you can take.

Using a library is a skill anyone can learn—and in most cases, it's a skill you had a little while back and can relearn fast. Just think of the tips below as a quick refresher on how to search library catalogs, how to navigate Subject Headings and call numbers, and how to prepare to visit a research library's special and unique collections. And soon enough, you'll be uncovering what you need for your own creative work, whether that's by visiting a fashion history library in person or by studying the digitized blueprint photograms of botanist Anna Atkins via a library's online offerings.

At most libraries, a catalog provides the primary way to discover what that particular library has in its collections. Most library catalogs are available online to anyone to search, and you'll usually find a link to your library's catalog on its home page. Library catalogs vary from institution to institution, but the guidance below applies in most cases. (Some libraries still have and use low-tech alternatives to online catalogs—files of cards, or printed books describing the library's holdings; these legacy guides can be useful as well, and I touch on these below, after an overview of online catalogs.)

Think of a library catalog as a giant online database with searchable entries called catalog records describing each and every book in a library's collection. Each book has its own catalog record, and that record holds certain information about the book to help you decide if it has what you're searching for. Librarians past and present have created these catalog records, and each record offers an excellent starting point to judge whether you should take a closer look at the source described. The elements of information used to describe a book in a catalog record will be arranged and displayed in different ways, depending on the library catalog you're using. But they generally include the following:

- Book title.
- Author Name: *formatted last, first.*
- Publication Details (sometimes called Imprint): *place of publication, publisher or printer name, year of publication.*
- Physical Description: *number of pages, how tall it is, and if it contains illustrations, a bibliography, or an index.*
- Library of Congress Subject Headings: *some subjects selected to describe what the book is about (more on these on page 36).*
- Call Number: *a combination of numbers and/or letters that tell you where on the shelf the book can be found (more on these on page 33).*

For example, one of the books that designer Gretchen Hirsch turned to in her study of millinery techniques is described this way in the catalog at New York Public Library, where she came to do her research:

| | |
|---|---|
| AUTHOR: | Garnell, Helene. |
| TITLE: | It's fun to make a hat, by Helene Garnell. |
| IMPRINT: | New York: Liveright Publishing Corporation [1944]. |
| DESCRIPTION: | 114 [13] p. illus., diagrs. 27 x 21 cm. |
| SUBJECT: | Millinery. |
| CALL NUMBER: | MMV (Garnell, H. It's fun to make a hat) |

Because entire catalog records once had to fit onto small index cards (before things moved to the online environment), they're full of abbreviations that might seem a bit opaque to you at times. Here are explanations of the most common ones:

n.p. = *no place of publication / publisher given*

n.d. = *no date of publication given*

p. = *pages*

illus. = *contains illustrations*

col. illus. = *contains illustrations in color*

diagrs. = *contains diagrams*

pl. = *contains plates ( full-page illustrations)*

Each of the elements in a catalog record is a clue that helps you to know if you should track down that book to see if it has what you want. For example, when designer Liesl Gibson was hunting for illustrated texts on soil and geology, looking at each catalog record to confirm that it was illustrated was as easy as finding "illus." in the description. And when identifying books on stencil design from the Arts and Crafts era, artist Anna Bondoc looked at the date of publication of each volume, to be sure the books fell within that time period. And, by keeping an eye on Subject Headings in catalog records, artist Molly Schnick was able to focus her research specifically on books that cover Japanese traditions by finding those with the Subject Heading "Heraldry—Japan."

Remember that a resource's catalog record provides a starting point, but it can't tell the complete story (because of the complex history of evolving research priorities and terminology in libraries). Sometimes you need to see the resource itself to see if it's useful. If you're searching for images of octopuses, for example, you might need to look through a number of books that are categorized by the Subject Heading "Aquatic Animals" in order to find the ones with octopuses. The catalog record probably won't tell you in advance if a particular animal is included in a particular volume, but it will let you know if you're in the right subject area.

The most important thing to remember, when it comes to call numbers, is that you should take note of a book's call number if you're going to want to find that book on the shelf or order it from a closed stack area (for more on closed and open stacks, see page 23). The second most important thing to remember about them is that, at least in libraries with open stacks where you can browse the bookshelves on your own, a call number scheme works to place books on similar topics on the shelves near one another, so if you go to a library shelf to look for one particular book on vernacular architecture (a topic that graphic designer Sarah Goldschadt browsed while designing her paper houses), chances are that you'll find other books on the shelf before and after it that you also might like. In closed stack libraries this won't apply, because call number systems are devised to maximize shelf space, not to place books on similar subjects together; and since you can't browse their shelves it doesn't matter.

Different libraries use different call number systems. The two most common schemes you'll find are Library of Congress Classification (LCC) and Dewey Decimal Classification (DDC). It's worth knowing a bit about each, but by no means do you need to memorize any numbers or letters. Think of the following guidance as comparable to glancing over the map of a city you're about to visit so you'll know the basic lay of the land—not to memorize every street name but to get a general sense of direction and a few landmarks to get you started.

DDC has been commonly used for over a century, and it's often found in public libraries and neighborhood libraries. DDC divides works into ten distinct categories and assigns each category a numeric range:

00-099 Computer Science, Information & General Works
100-199 Philosophy & Psychology
200-299 Religion
300-399 Social Sciences
400-499 Language
500-599 Science
600-699 Technology
700-799 Arts & Recreation
800-899 Literature
900-999 History & Geography

Winfield Public Library

Within each of these large categories, topics are given more specific number assignments so that books on the same topics are shelved together. Here are a couple of examples of DDC classifications that I often browse at my public library:

700-799: Arts & Recreation
740-749: Drawing & Decorative Arts
746: Textile Arts

600-699: Technology
640-649: Home Economics & Family Living
646: Sewing, Clothing, Personal Living

So if you find yourself in a library that uses DDC and you want to find books on sewing clothing, you'll end up looking at books with 646 call numbers.

The second common scheme you might encounter is Library of Congress Classification (LCC). LCC was created as a means of classifying the collection at the Library of Congress, but it has been adopted by many academic and research libraries over the years. In LCC, the broadest classes number twenty-one, as opposed to DDC's ten.

A   General Works
B   Philosophy, Psychology, and Religion
C   Auxiliary Sciences of History
D   General and Old World History
E   History of America
F   History of the United States and British, Dutch, French, and Latin America
G   Geography, Anthropology, and Recreation
H   Social Sciences
J   Political Science

K   Law
L   Education
M   Music
N   Fine Arts
P   Language and Literature
Q   Science
R   Medicine
S   Agriculture
T   Technology
U   Military Science
V   Naval Science
Z   Bibliography, Library Science, and General Information Resources

Like DDC, each broad class is further divided into more specific subclasses, using a combination of letters and numbers to designate specific subjects. Here are a couple of examples:

N: Fine Arts
    NK: Decorative Arts
        NK8800-9505.5: Textiles
T: Technology
    TT: Handicrafts, Arts & Crafts
        TT490-695: Clothing Manufacture, Dressmaking, Tailoring

As a result, if you're researching dressmaking in a library that uses LCC, you'll end up browsing the section with call numbers between TT490 and TT695.

Here are a few examples of how books my contributors and I turned to in our research would be classified at libraries using these two different systems:

In the process of consulting reference sources when preparing my watermark-inspired pillows, I used books that you'd find under Z237 at a library using LCC system, and under 095 at a library that uses DDC. You'd find more books of animal illustrations like the one Grace Bonney used to create her votive holders under LCC class QL41, and under DDC class 769.432. When searching for cookbooks like those I consulted in preparing my cuts of meat embroideries, I could look under LCC class TX717, or under DDC class 641.59.

You'll find that both DDC and LCC call numbers will be a bit longer in practice, with some additional numbers or letters tacked onto the end. These provide more fine-grained information (letters of an author's last name, or year of publication, for instance) so that the book can be shelved (and found by you) in its proper place. In every case, just remember that the call number is like a book's address on the shelf and it's worth noting it down in its complete form so you can find it later.

DDC and LCC are by no means the only classification schemes you might encounter at a library. In fact, some libraries (including the research collections of New York Public Library, where I work) use their own unique call numbering systems you won't find anywhere else. As a user of such a library, you can think of the process of familiarizing yourself with these unique systems as an adventure; the more you explore it, the more you'll know your way around. By all means, however, ask for assistance; the librarians at such institutions will likely be extra helpful in getting you oriented since they know that users haven't ever encountered their system elsewhere.

And at closed stack libraries, where you can't do your own browsing and instead you place orders for books and a staff member gets them for you, you might see call numbers that don't correspond to subjects at all. Since you can't visit the shelves yourself, it doesn't matter in what order these books are placed on the storage shelves. In closed stack libraries the call number may be strictly a location code, with books shelved behind the scenes according to their size or according to when they were acquired.

So, what about catalogs that aren't online? Older libraries may have complex histories of collecting and cataloging, and as a result not every card file or printed collection description may have yet made it into an online catalog environment. Often at local neighborhood libraries you'll find everything in the online catalog; but research libraries are another matter. For some parts of collections at research libraries, a librarian may invite you to flip through low-tech card files or printed collections guides. Using these legacy guides will take you to a deeper level of research than your project might require, but it's worth knowing that they are still in use at some places.

## MORE ABOUT LIBRARY OF CONGRESS SUBJECT HEADINGS

Library of Congress Subject Headings (I'll call them Subject Headings for short) are like the keys to the kingdom when searching a library catalog. They are selected words or phrases that identify what a book is about, and you might think of them as a highly refined set of tags applied to books or magazines to guide you to the materials that will help you in your specific research project. You'll usually find a few Subject Headings somewhere near the bottom of every catalog record.

Subject Headings all start out quite broad, but each can be given finer focus by the use of what are called subdivisions. Subdivisions can narrow things down by topic, form, time period, and place. Here are some examples of subdivisions applied to Subject Headings:

EMBROIDERY—HISTORY. (*narrows down a broader subject*)
EMBROIDERY—HANDBOOKS, MANUALS, ETC. (*indicates book's format;
    other useful form subdivisions to know are "Pictorial Works" and "Illustrations"*)
EMBROIDERY—EARLY WORKS TO 1800. (*narrows down to works printed
    during specific time periods*)
EMBROIDERY—JAPAN. (*identifies specific geographic region*)

When embroidery artist Mary Corbet was hunting for examples of elaborate decorative handwriting, she looked at books with the Subject Heading "Penmanship" and then dug deeper by focusing just on those works classified as "Penmanship—Specimens." This subdivision allowed her to focus her time just on books that included illustrations of penmanship examples.

Subject Headings were created so that a library user could find books in a library's catalog according to a research topic, and they provided critical guidance at a time before keyword searching became possible. They're still invaluable, and I explain below how you can use them to find what you need while searching a library catalog.

The Library of Congress Subject Heading system has been in use since 1898, but it grows and changes in response to shifts in cultural trends. Between six and eight thousand Subject Headings are added or updated each year. Keep in mind that Subject Headings are not created prescriptively, but only as a response to a growing body of published materials on a certain topic or a shift in common ways to describe a topic. For example, we might use a word like sewists today, but it is not included in Library of Congress Subject Headings. Not yet, that is; as more publications include the word, sewists just might get their very own Subject Heading!

## HOW TO SEARCH A LIBRARY CATALOG

Keyword searching, which looks for a certain word or words across multiple fields, is the kind of searching you're probably most familiar with today—it's what you do when you enter a word or phrase into a search engine. Library catalogs let you do a keyword search as well; the keyword search will work differently, from catalog to catalog, but usually it searches for the keyword you've entered in each of the major elements in a catalog record, like author, title, and Subject Headings. But when you combine a keyword search along with a Subject Heading search, you can uncover materials that may be older, more obscure, and loaded with potential inspiration. Why bother using both keyword and Subject Heading searches? New book titles often contain all of the relevant keywords you might think to search for, so a keyword search will lead you to these without too much effort. But publishers and printers a century ago didn't think that way, and their book titles and subtitles might not reveal the whole story of what a book is about. For example, the book title *Toy Book* (an iconic 1972 kids' creative activity book by Steven Caney) doesn't make it obvious that it'll be a how-to guide for kids to make their own toys. Additionally, the words publishers and printers and authors use to describe topics often change over time. As a result, some books might not come up in a keyword search if they use obscure or archaic terms or if they are written in a language other than English. And sometimes a keyword search can lead to results you *don't* want, simply because the keyword you searched for is somewhere in the catalog record.

But by harnessing the power of Subject Headings along with keyword searching in a library catalog, you can discover what you want and also weed out what you don't want. Here's an approach I recommend to researchers just getting started who want to find out what Subject Headings might be useful:

Say you want to learn more about Irish lace. You might start with a keyword search for Irish AND lace, and the search results might include the following book titles:

*Lab Coats and Lace: The Lives and Legacies of Inspiring Irish Women Scientists and Pioneers* / edited by Mary Mulvihill. Dublin: WITS, 2009.

*Irish Lace* / Candace McCarthy. A Zebra Historical Romance. New York, NY: Kensington Pub. Corp., 2001.

These two titles, with science and romance at their hearts, are not about lace making, alas. There's also this title:

*Irish Lace* / Ada Longfield. Dublin: Eason, 1978.

You can't really tell anything about what this might be about, based only on its author and title. But if you read through the rest of the book's catalog record, you see that it's been given the Subject Heading "Lace and Lace Making—Ireland" and you now know that it might be a good book to browse. You've also successfully identified one of the official Subject Headings that covers your topic.

Keep looking at the list of results of your keyword search, noting the Subject Headings that have been assigned to each title. You'll quickly see how Subject Headings help you to figure out which titles to ignore and which ones hold real promise. And you might find some more Subject Headings worth remembering for your research. For instance, the following titles have been assigned the Subject Heading "Irish Crochet Lace" in their records by the Library of Congress.

*Designs and Instructions for Irish Crochet Lace*. T. Buettner & Co., Inc. Chicago, New York, etc.: Buettner & Co., Inc., 1912.

*The Priscilla Irish Crochet Book*. Boston, MA.: The Priscilla Publishing Company, 1909.

After you feel like you've gotten a few good Subject Headings to start with, the next step is to shift from a keyword search to a Subject Heading search. Sometimes library catalogs will include a Subject Heading search option on their basic search page, but you might also find it as an option under an advanced or extended search page.

Different library catalogs have different features. In some catalogs, a Subject Heading Search will immediately yield a list of books assigned to that particular Subject Heading. But in another catalog, the result might instead be a list of Subject Headings, one of which will be the one for which you searched. For example, a Subject Heading search for "Lace and Lace Making—Ireland" might yield results that display your exact search, nested alphabetically among other Subject Headings:

> Lace and Lace Making—India.
> Lace and Lace Making—Ireland.
> Lace and Lace Making—Ireland—Dublin.
> Lace and Lace Making—Ireland—Limerick.
> Lace and Lace Making—Ireland—Limerick (Limerick)—Patterns.
> Lace and Lace Making—Israel.
> Lace and Lace Making—Italy.

Usually, each of these Subject Headings will be a live link that, when clicked, takes you to a list of titles that are each about this specific topic. As a result, a Subject Heading search accomplishes two key steps in your research: It introduces you to other Subject Headings that might interest you, and it offers you a list of titles on the specific Subject Heading for which you searched.

One element you might notice, in a list of Subject Headings that results from a Subject Heading search, is suggestions of other Subject Headings that aren't close neighbors, alphabetically. These suggestions are there to guide you to other Subject Headings that you might not have found otherwise. For instance, the results of a Subject Heading search for "Handicraft" will include some "narrower terms" like "Quillwork" and "Industrial Arts." It will recommend as well that you "see also" some other Subject Headings like "Manual Training" or "Occupations." If your Subject Heading search yields "narrower term" or "see also" suggestions, it's always interesting and often fruitful to browse them to uncover what you might have missed. In fact, it is just such a "see also" Subject Heading (Manual Training) that led to the book that inspired crafter Brett Bara to create her textbook-inspired soft pyramids project.

Beyond keywords and Subject Heading searches, though, there are other ways to make the catalog work for you. Here are some ideas:

*Focus on materials published during a particular time period:*
Perhaps you're interested in finding some old images of birds to use as a basis for some quilt appliques. You might start as described on pages 37-39, with a keyword search (birds) and then find your way to a Subject Heading search ("Birds—Pictorial Works"). But if you're at a large library, the resulting titles still make for a pretty long list. What if you narrowed your search by date? If your library catalog offers an advanced or expanded search option by date of publication, you can add a date range to your Subject Heading search, and then only get books that were published during a specific time period. You can, alternatively, simply sort your results by date of publication and then look at the portion of the list that includes the years of publication that interest you.

Narrowing your results to works published before 1923 is an easy way to limit your sources to those in the public domain. By looking through the results of your search for items published in the United States from this time period, you'll quickly identify materials free from copyright restrictions and ready for you to adapt and reuse. (For more details on the ins and outs of copyright, see page 55.)

*Look just for magazines, instead of books:*
If you're searching for vintage magazines, journals, and newspapers, the library catalog is still a good starting point. Most library catalogs allow you, as an advanced or expanded search option, to search specifically for magazines (they might call it a Journals search or a Periodicals search); this type of search weeds out any book titles, leading to a more focused list.

*Find materials with less common formats, like maps, prints, and handwritten letters:*
Many catalogs' advanced or expanded search options allow you to limit your search to specific formats like maps or graphics collections. Some library catalogs also include descriptive information on manuscript collections and other less common materials. Start with the catalog and see what you can discover. But keep in mind that less common formats like these are often managed differently from library to library, and if you see yourself being drawn to these kinds of special collections, the best step is to reach out to a librarian who can help you to learn more about them and then gain access to them.

*Let the catalog track your progress:*

Modern library catalogs offer more personalized features than ever before, so make use of whatever online tools are helpful to you. You may be able to use your library card to create an account in the library catalog online where you can save favorite searches or build and export book lists. If your library catalog doesn't offer these features, it's best to do the unglamorous work of keeping a pencil and notebook handy to make notes on what you've searched and discovered. Good record keeping, though admittedly less exciting than paging through an eighteenth-century volume of hand-colored fishes, will allow you to keep tabs on the ground you've covered so you can revisit favorite sources.

*Let bibliographies guide you in your searches:*

A bibliography in the back of a book—or an entire book that is just a bibliography—can provide an ingenious shortcut to finding what you want. In a good bibliography, its creator has recorded and recommended works that he or she has found on a certain topic. So, if you find a bibliography on a topic that interests you, spend a bit of time seeing what it contains. Think of it as the author having done some of the legwork for you. To find bibliographies on a topic, figure out what Subject Heading you want to use and then add the subdivision "Bibliography" to it. For example, a book with the Subject Heading "Insects—Pictorial Works—Bibliography" will give you concrete guidance to recommended illustrated works on insects.

*Let other books guide you in your searches:*

Another way to begin to build a search strategy is to identify promising Subject Headings by looking inside a newish book you already have and like on the topic that interests you. Often in books published in recent decades you'll find what's called Cataloging-in-Publication Data on the book's copyright page. This data includes the Subject Headings that have been assigned to that particular book by the Library of Congress in advance of its publication. By seeing what Subject Headings have been assigned to a book you already like, you can then do a Subject Heading search in the library catalog for other books with that same Subject Heading.

## LOOKING BEYOND A SINGLE LIBRARY

Have you exhausted all the possibilities at your favorite local library? Or are you planning a trip and want to look into potential library stops at your destination? Perhaps you want to find out which libraries around the world have the kinds of materials that interest you. Here are some ideas for taking that next step:

*Union Catalogs Online*

Union catalogs do just what it sounds like they do: They unify the holdings of many different libraries in a single online database. These catalogs are an invaluable means of quickly finding out which library—whether near or far—has a specific book you want to see. One giant in the world of union catalogs is WorldCat (www.worldcat.org). Others include Copac in the United Kingdom (http://copac.ac.uk/), AMICUS in Canada (www.collectionscanada. gc.ca/amicus), and Trove in Australia (http://trove.nla.gov.au). And you can browse more union catalog options at the "Other Union Catalogues Directory" maintained by the Serials Union Catalogue for the UK (www.suncat.ac.uk/other.shtml).

*Interlibrary Loan and Document Delivery*

If you've found in WorldCat that the book you want is too far away for you to visit it, don't despair. You may still be able to consult it at your home institution, if both your library and the library that has the materials you want participate in an interlibrary loan program. Interlibrary loan programs differ from place to place, but the central idea is that your library works on your behalf to borrow a book from another library. Think of it as the book coming to you so that you don't have to go to the book. Many rare, fragile, or historical materials will not be candidates for interlibrary loan, but once you've got specific questions about materials be sure to ask what might be possible at your favorite nearby library.

Another service that your library might offer is document delivery, which is an alternative to interlibrary loan in which scans of pages of a work come to you. This is useful when you need to read just a single article or an individual chapter of a book held in another library. Your library might participate in such a program, and it's worth asking about.

*LibGuides*

Another way to make the most of what libraries and librarians all over have to offer is to visit the LibGuides Community (http://community.libguides.com). LibGuides are online research assistance sites, created by librarians to lead their readers to sources on all sorts of subjects. Every LibGuide is customized by the librarian who creates it to address her readers' specific needs (and often to meet coursework requirements if it is a university library's LibGuide), so each one is going to be different. But often they include features like suggested Subject Headings and call number ranges, as well as recommended books, bibliographies, Web resources, and more. Some LibGuides are private—which means that only one particular library's users can view them—but thousands are publicly accessible. At the LibGuides Community, you can search for all the freely available ones by keyword.

## THE WORLD OF
# DIGITAL LIBRARIES

*Maybe you're like me, and you tend to become curious* about things at odd hours of the night when libraries are closed. At such moments, and at lots of other moments every day as well, I turn to digital libraries. Always open and always ready to offer up surprising sources, digital libraries gather and present vast amounts of materials in novel ways. You might find a timeline dotted with documents and images relevant to a particular place and time, or digital exhibitions providing context and narrative around a body of materials, or something completely unexpected, such as a series of haunting daguerreotypes of women knitting (from the Houghton Library's Department of Printing and Graphic Arts, Harvard University), which I found when searching the Digital Public Library of America.

I've surprised people at times with my love for digital libraries, because they assume that a rare book librarian like me should have room in her heart only for paper, hand-stitched bindings, and ink squash. And it's true that I love books as physical artifacts, with each handmade volume bearing evidence of how it was made and how it has been used. It is, after all, the handcrafted nature of books that drew me to the field. But I adore digital libraries for their superpowers: They allow me to discover and browse collections that I might otherwise never be able to experience; they enable me to search and analyze collections in new ways; and they invite me to collaborate with others, compare materials, and share my discoveries.

If you remain skeptical that using digital libraries should be part of your inspiration-gathering routine online, you may be interested to know that well over half the projects in this book came to be because of access to digitized sources. Early natural history illustrations, landmark photography, children's textbooks, hand-drawn maps, propaganda posters, historical marbled papers, handwriting and type design specimens, cookbook illustrations, or botanical studies—just about anything you seek, and more, can be found in digital libraries.

Following are details on several digital libraries that have a lot to offer any crafter interested in discovering design inspiration online, plus by a few tips on how to use digital libraries.

**Digital Public Library of America**   http://dp.la
Like an "extraordinary digital attic," the DPLA offers a single place to search, discover, and explore the incredible variety of digitized collections that are maintained on individual platforms by individual libraries, archives, and museums around the country. What I love about the DPLA platform is how it allows me to discover digitized collections I might not otherwise think to search for. In fact, it was the DPLA that led me to World War II poster collections that I recommend as a source for World War II–era graphics (on page 195). Its expanding list of partners includes some of the biggest providers of digitized library content online, including the Smithsonian Institution, the Biodiversity Heritage Library, the National Archives, and the New York Public Library.

**Internet Archive**   http://archive.org
Offering full access to texts, audio, moving images, software, and archived Web pages in its ever-expanding collections, the Internet Archive is another digital giant worth exploring. For printed books in digital form as well as cultural artifacts of all media, this is a key resource. It features a way to build your own bookmarked list of favorite sources, to add comments, and to contribute to the user forum as well.

**Open Library**   http://openlibrary.org
This project of the Internet Archive seeks to build a free public online catalog of the entire universe of books. Many are also available for browsing and reading online through their site.

**Hathi Trust Digital Library**   http://www.hathitrust.org
Created as a digital preservation repository by an international community of nearly one hundred research libraries, Hathi Trust Digital Library offers access to millions of public domain and in-copyright books via a user-friendly platform. And if you are a member of one of the partner institutions (generally this means that you have library privileges at one of the participant libraries, which are listed on the site), you have extensive downloading privileges. But even if you are not a member of a partner institution, you can still browse and discover sources, read them online, and download some materials.

**Flickr Commons**   www.flickr.com/commons

This rich resource, hosted by Flickr, brings together images from public photography archives and libraries worldwide. With dozens of institutions contributing images of all kinds, it's a variety-filled visual treat to explore and a fun way to discover institutions and collections you might never have known about before. And as with Flickr generally, you can tag and label things to help you to remember them.

**World Digital Library**   www.wdl.org/en

This global, multilingual collaboration of many libraries, archives, and cultural institutions was designed to share primary source materials from around the world. Materials range from musical scores to maps, books to prints, and photographs to architectural drawings. It was developed by the Library of Congress, in collaboration with cultural institutions worldwide, with the support of the United Nations Education, Scientific, and Cultural Organization (UNESCO).

**Europeana**   www.europeana.eu

Europeana offers a single starting point for searching and discovering millions of digitized books, paintings, films, objects, and primary source materials held in institutions across Europe.

**European Library**   www.theeuropeanlibrary.org/tel4

This portal to the collections of forty-eight national libraries of Europe includes the holdings of key European research libraries.

**Digital Book Index**   www.digitalbookindex.org/about.htm

This site indexes the sites where you can find over 140,000 freely available digitized books from publishers, universities and libraries, and private enterprises. You can browse and search in different ways, including by subject, author, and title.

**Google Books**   books.google.com

Perhaps the most familiar trove of public domain materials, Google Books is hindered in its usefulness by its limited search functions. Google's admittedly powerful keyword search doesn't allow you to focus your search options to just author name or book title or Subject Heading, for example. It remains a very useful resource, however, for serendipitous browsing. And if you see a digitized book that interests you, you can find out what library holds the original copy by visiting the book's "About" page and scrolling to the bottom to read the bibliographic information. You can also build your own online library of books to which you want to return in the future.

In addition to these big, sprawling digital libraries that offer digitized materials from a variety of institutions, there are many finely focused sources created by individual libraries that are equally worth exploring. I have my favorites among these smaller, focused digital collections, which I think you'll like, too. Turn to page 48 to learn more about these in Recommended Library Collections.

Ready to get started exploring the digital libraries described on pages 45-46? Here are some tips on how you might use them:

- Get a glimpse inside a book to see if it's a source you want to spend more time with (thumbnail views offered on most sites are the online equivalent of flipping through a whole text quickly).

- Study a book's illustrations to decide if they have the sort of images you seek.

- If you've seen a book listed as being physically available in a library but you can't get to it in person, search an online library to see if it's been digitized.

- Search entire texts for certain words or phrases in an instant (often the entirety of a book will have been made keyword searchable).

- Focus on materials that have entered the public domain, which are freely available for adapting and reusing in your designs (always check the permissions policies on each site to see what rights issues might exist, and turn to page 55 to learn more about copyright).

- If the digital library you're using offers it, create an account so you can flag, bookmark, tag, or otherwise collect and gather notes on sources you discover so you can find your way back to them quickly in the future.

# LIBRARY COLLECTIONS

*As a librarian at the New York Public Library,* I spend most of my time learning about my own library's research collections so that I can assist readers who use our materials and those who write in with questions. But part of my time is also spent getting to know other institutions' collections, so that I can help my readers by referring them to other libraries that might have the materials they need for their work.

As a result, I know a little about quite a few collections, and I've developed a list of favorite go-to libraries on a number of design, book arts, and handicraft topics. In this section, I present my list augmented with suggestions from librarians around the country. I've emphasized collections with substantial digital presences, so that no matter where you live you can take advantage of their offerings. But remember, if you happen to live near any of these research libraries, you can reach out to them to ask if you might visit in person. (See page 28 for tips on planning to visit a research library in person.)

If you'd like to uncover more library collections that match your specific interests, turn to page 26 for guidance on identifying libraries. Additionally, another good way to discover which libraries have the kinds of materials you want is to start poking around in large digital libraries (see page 43 for more on these) for materials that interest you. Usually digitized sources will cite the location of the original material; seeing these locations will give you a sense of additional library collections of possible interest, and from there you can visit a particular library's website and search for more information on what they offer.

## GENERAL VISUAL RESOURCES

**BIBLIODYSSEY (DIGITAL ONLY)**
This frequently updated blog posts visually inspiring images of historical materials from libraries on a variety of topics. http://bibliodyssey.blogspot.com

**BRITISH LIBRARY, LONDON, UK**
Images Online provides an online portal to discover the visual riches held at this library.
https://imagesonline.bl.uk

**NEW YORK PUBLIC LIBRARY, NEW YORK, NY**
NYPL's Digital Gallery is the digital starting point for image research for all kinds of materials throughout the institution's collections. www.digitalgallery.nypl.org

**SMITHSONIAN INSTITUTION LIBRARIES, WASHINGTON, DC**
The Galaxy of Images is a great starting point online to begin to discover the visual materials throughout this institution's collections. www.sil.si.edu/imagegalaxy

**PUBLIC DOMAIN REVIEW (DIGITAL ONLY)**
This site highlights literary and visual sources now in the public domain on a broad range of subjects (and often these materials can be found in digital libraries).
http://publicdomainreview.org

## HOME ECONOMICS

**MANN LIBRARY, CORNELL UNIVERSITY, ITHACA, NY**
Hearth: A Digital Archive of Home Economics Publications, 1850–1925, provides digital access to early books, pamphlets, and visual materials related to domestic economies. http://hearth.library.cornell.edu/h/hearth/index.html

**UNIVERSITY OF WISCONSIN LIBRARIES, MADISON, WI**
The Human Ecology Collections Online includes a range of materials, such as publications on dressmaking, millinery, cooking, and even playing house.
http://uwdc.library.wisc.edu/collections/HumanEcol

**SALLIE BINGHAM CENTER FOR WOMEN'S HISTORY AND CULTURE, DUKE UNIVERSITY LIBRARIES, DURHAM, NC**
Glory of Women: An Introduction to Prescriptive Literature highlights and contextualizes the library's collection of books that sought to advise women on home economics, beauty, etiquette, handicrafts, marriage, and more. http://library.duke.edu/rubenstein/bingham/guides/glory/index.html

**HARVARD UNIVERSITY LIBRARIES, CAMBRIDGE, MA**
Women Working, 1800–1930, is an online starting point to explore manuscripts, photographs, trade catalogs, and other materials that illuminate women's role in the American economy. http://ocp.hul.harvard.edu/ww

## CRAFT HISTORY AND CULTURE

**ANTIQUE PATTERN LIBRARY (DIGITAL ONLY)**
This digital library offers public domain handicraft books and patterns on a variety of topics, including needlecraft, beading, knitting, lace, quilting, ribbonwork, and more.
www.antiquepatternlibrary.org/html/warm/main.htm

**HUNTER LIBRARY, WESTERN CAROLINA UNIVERSITY, CULLOWHEE, NC**
North Carolina's Craft Revival History provides a digital means to explore the state's handmade material culture, in partnership with institutions including the John C. Campbell Folk School and the Penland School of Crafts.
www.wcu.edu/craftrevival/index.htm

**AMERICAN CRAFT COUNCIL LIBRARY, MINNEAPOLIS, MN**
The research library of the American Craft Council maintains print and visual works related to American craft as well as artist files (and a portion of its library collection is online). www.craftcouncil.org/library

**LIBRARY OF CONGRESS, WASHINGTON, DC**
The American Folklife Center documents and records stories and works of handmade material culture around the country, including quilting traditions, handmade tools, vernacular architecture, and folk art. You can read more about the Center's work online.
www.loc.gov/folklife/guide/materialculture.html

## PRINTED EPHEMERA

**HAGLEY MUSEUM AND LIBRARY, WILMINGTON, DE**
Roadside America Postcards, 1930–1960, includes depictions of iconic American roadside architecture online. http://digital.hagley.org/cdm/landingpage/collection/p268001coll21

**NEW YORK PUBLIC LIBRARY, NEW YORK, NY**
What's on the Menu? allows you to browse, read, and even help to transcribe the library's collection of historical menus online. http://menus.nypl.org/

**LILLY LIBRARY, INDIANA UNIVERSITY, BLOOMINGTON, IN**
The Victorian Valentines Collection includes a variety of forms and styles popular during this time.
www.indiana.edu/~liblilly/valentines/valentine.html

**WINTERTHUR MUSEUM, GARDEN, AND LIBRARY, WILMINGTON, DE**
Digital Collections shared by Winterthur include eighteenth-century playing cards and nineteenth-century French candy wrappers. www.winterthur.org/?p=565

**BODLEIAN LIBRARY, UNIVERSITY OF OXFORD, OXFORD, UK**
The John Johnson Collection of Printed Ephemera presents a portion of its collection online, organized by various topics, including Cats and Crime.
www.bodleian.ox.ac.uk/johnson/jj-images/galleries

## BOOK ARTS AND BOOKBINDINGS

**UNIVERSITY OF TORONTO LIBRARIES, TORONTO, CANADA**
British Armorial Bindings gathers in a single digital database all heraldic devices applied by British book owners to their book bindings. The devices can be browsed by individual visual elements found in coats of arms, including anchors, crows, salamanders, unicorns, and ships. http://armorial.library.utoronto.ca

**PUBLISHERS' CLOTH BINDINGS (DIGITAL ONLY)**
This visual catalog of nineteenth-century decorative cloth bindings can be browsed by style (Arts and Crafts, Eastlake, and Art Deco, for example) or by historical or literary theme. The cloth binding designs provide rich inspiration today in both pattern and color.
http://bindings.lib.ua.edu/index.html

**BOSTON ATHENAEUM, BOSTON, MA**
This library's Inventory of Bookbinders' Finishing Tools is a carefully detailed record of each historical brass finishing tool in the library's care, its provenance if known, and the design that tool makes.
www.bostonathenaeum.org/node/811

**FOLGER SHAKESPEARE LIBRARY, WASHINGTON, DC**
The Bindings Image Collection provides online access to images and descriptive details of historical bindings. It can be searched by place, time, person, and text.
http://luna.folger.edu/luna/servlet/BINDINGS~1~1

**BRITISH LIBRARY, LONDON, UK**
The British Library's Bindings Database acts as a visual online finding aid to selections of fine bindings from that library's wide-ranging collection as well as from partner institutions. www.bl.uk/catalogues/bookbindings

**PRINCETON UNIVERSITY LIBRARY, PRINCETON, NJ**
Hand Bookbindings is an illuminating and visually appealing digital exhibition that uses images of books from the library's collections to illustrate the various elements used in binding and decorating a book by hand. It includes beautiful examples of embroidered bindings, edge decorations, and endleaves.
http://libweb5.princeton.edu/visual_materials/hb/index.html

**UNIVERSITY OF WASHINGTON LIBRARY, SEATTLE, WA**
The Decorative and Decorated Papers Collection provides historical information as well as digitized specimens of both historical and modern papers online.
http://content.lib.washington.edu/dpweb

**NATIONAL LIBRARY OF THE NETHERLANDS, DEN HAAG, NETHERLANDS**
The Decorated Papers Digital Exhibition offers examples of decorated papers online and includes information on the history of the art as well as contemporary artists' interpretations.
www.kb.nl/en/web-exhibitions/decorated-paper

## COSTUME AND FASHION

**METROPOLITAN MUSEUM OF ART COSTUME INSTITUTE, NEW YORK, NY & BROOKLYN MUSEUM COSTUME COLLECTION, BROOKLYN, NY**
The Shared Image Database allows you to see images of more than 30,000 items held in these two institutions. You can narrow your search by place, time, creator, or material. For example, you can search only for items created by Elsa Schiaparelli in wool, if you want.
www.metmuseum.org/collections/search-the-collections?deptids=62%7c8&ft=*

**FASHION INSTITUTE OF TECHNOLOGY, NEW YORK, NY**
FIT Special Collections and Archives maintains design archives as well as vintage printed works, and some drawings and sketches can be viewed online.
www.fitnyc.edu/8412.asp

**CHICAGO HISTORY MUSEUM, CHICAGO, IL**
Their Costume and Textile Collection includes more than 50,000 items of clothing and accesories, and their digital image inventory continues to grow.
www.chicagohs.org/research/aboutcollection/costumes

## ARTS AND DESIGN

**GETTY RESEARCH INSTITUTE LIBRARY, LOS ANGELES, CA**
Getty Portal offers a wide variety of digitized foundational reference sources and other invaluable texts on art, architecture, material culture, and related topics.
http://portal.getty.edu/portal/landing

**COOPER-HEWITT NATIONAL DESIGN LIBRARY, SMITHSONIAN LIBRARIES, NEW YORK, NY**
Design and decorative arts are broadly documented in collections of trade catalogs, periodicals, patterns, books, ephemera, and archival materials.
http://library.si.edu/libraries/cooper-hewitt

**COOPER-HEWITT NATIONAL DESIGN MUSEUM, SMITHSONIAN INSTITUTION, NEW YORK, NY**
In addition to the library (described above), this museum's collection search page offers stimulating ways to explore images of the institution's objects, textiles, and art (including searching by color!).
http://collection.cooperhewitt.org/

**ARCHIVE OF ART AND DESIGN, VICTORIA AND ALBERT MUSEUM, LONDON, UK**
This archive includes materials on embroidery, textiles, wallpaper, knitting, and more. Selected materials can be viewed online.
www.vam.ac.uk/page/a/archive-of-art-and-design

**MODERN GRAPHIC HISTORY LIBRARY, WASHINGTON UNIVERSITY, ST. LOUIS, MO**
Dedicated to modern American illustration and pictorial graphic culture, this collection includes original art and personal papers as well as books, magazines, advertisements, graphic novels, comics, posters, and animation. Selections can be browsed online.
http://library.wustl.edu/units/spec/MGHL

## CHILDREN'S BOOKS

**GEORGE A. SMATHERS LIBRARIES, UNIVERSITY OF FLORIDA, GAINESVILLE, FL**
The Baldwin Library of Historic Children's Literature contains more than 100,000 British and American publications for children. Many have been digitized and can be viewed online. http://ufdc.ufl.edu/?c=juv

**FREE LIBRARY OF PHILADELPHIA, PHILADELPHIA, PA**
The Free Library's Children's Book and Illustrator Collections span the seventeenth- to the twentieth-centuries, and include early printed editions as well as original artworks by Beatrix Potter, Robert Lawson, Kate Greenaway, and other artists.
http://libwww.freelibrary.org/rarebooks/coll_children.cfm

**UNIVERSITY OF PITTSBURGH'S UNIVERSITY LIBRARY SYSTEM, PITTSBURGH, PA**
The 19th Century Schoolbooks project presents selections from the library's Nietz Old Textbook Collection, as well as reference sources and bibliographies.
http://digital.library.pitt.edu/nietz

**PRINCETON UNIVERSITY LIBRARY, PRINCETON, NJ**
The Cotsen Children's Library contains historical books, manuscripts, toys, illustrations, and original children's book art. Their site contains selected digitized materials presented as exhibitions for browsing.
www.princeton.edu/cotsen

**SAN FRANCISCO PUBLIC LIBRARY, SAN FRANCISCO, CA**
The George M. Fox Collection of Early Children's Books includes toy books, movable books, and colorful illustrated works, some of which (like *Miss Mouser's Tea Party* and *The Ark Alphabet*) can be viewed online. http://sfpl.org/index.php?pg=2000003201

**SALLIE BINGHAM CENTER FOR WOMEN'S HISTORY AND CULTURE, DUKE UNIVERSITY LIBRARIES, DURHAM, NC**
*Beyond Nancy Drew: A Guide to Girls' Literature* highlights the collection's holdings in books marketed to girls and young women, including detective novels, etiquette guides, and adventure novels. http://library.duke.edu/rubenstein/bingham/guides/beyond/index.html

**HARVARD UNIVERSITY LIBRARY, CAMBRIDGE, MA**
*Views of Readers, Readership, and Reading History* surveys how children learned to read in previous centuries and reproduces a variety of early readers, grammar primers, and textbooks. http://ocp.hul.harvard.edu/reading/textbooks.html

**LIBRARY OF CONGRESS, WASHINGTON, DC**
*Children's Literature* selections that can be viewed online have been arranged alphabetically by title, and the titles available include some iconic works (*The Secret Garden*) as well as unexpected treasures (*Ballad of the Lost Hare*). www.loc.gov/rr/rarebook/digitalcoll/digitalcoll-children.html

## MEDIEVAL MANUSCRIPTS

**WALTERS ART MUSEUM, BALTIMORE, MD**
This museum's early manuscripts and rare books online include early works from Armenian, Ethiopian, and Ottoman traditions. http://art.thewalters.org/browse/category/manuscript-and-rare-books

**UNIVERSITY OF PENNSYLVANIA RARE BOOK AND MANUSCRIPT LIBRARY, PHILADELPHIA, PA**
*Penn in Hand* offers digital images of selected medieval and renaissance manuscripts in its collections. http://dla.library.upenn.edu/dla/medren/index.html

**BRITISH LIBRARY, LONDON, UK**
The British Library's *Illuminated Manuscripts* is a virtual exhibition of manuscripts, organized around categories such as religious texts, the appearance of animals in illuminations, and Arthurian manuscripts. http://bl.uk/catalogues/illuminatedmanuscripts/tours.asp

**DIGITAL SCRIPTORIUM (DIGITAL ONLY)**
A multi-institutional collaboration, this project gathers and presents in a single site digital images of medieval and Renaissance manuscripts from around the United States and beyond. http://scriptorium.columbia.edu

## SCIENCE AND TECHNOLOGY

**BIODIVERSITY HERITAGE LIBRARY (DIGITAL ONLY)**
This consortium of natural history and botanical libraries makes foundational texts on the natural world openly available online. It offers a wealth of illustrated works on plants and animals. www.biodiversitylibrary.org

**UNITED STATES NATIONAL LIBRARY OF MEDICINE, BETHESDA, MD**
This library offers a variety of print and video materials from its collection online, including early books on the natural world. http://collections.nlm.nih.gov/muradora/welcome.jsp

**ROYAL SOCIETY LIBRARY, LONDON, UK**
The Royal Society Picture Library, which shares images from their collection of books, prints, and drawings, was established to inspire visitors to explore the visual history of science. https://pictures.royalsociety.org

**MEDICAL HERITAGE LIBRARY (DIGITAL ONLY)**
This collaboration among leading medical libraries around the world gathers and shares digital editions of historical medical texts. www.medicalheritage.org

**WILLIAM ANDREWS CLARK MEMORIAL LIBRARY, UCLA, LOS ANGELES, CA**
Although known for its eighteenth-century literary works, this library also has a strong history of science collection, with particular focus on natural philosophy and astronomy. http://clarklibrary.ucla.edu

**REANIMATION LIBRARY, BROOKLYN, NY**
This library, made up of an eclectic collection of outdated illustrated texts from previous decades on a variety of topics, selects book for their graphic content and their potential inspiration for artists and makers. www.reanimationlibrary.org

**WELLCOME LIBRARY, LONDON, UK**
This library, which holds more than 750,000 books, manuscripts, audio-visual materials, original art, and more, has created a digital image site with unexpected categories like tattoo art and Olympic sport illustrations, to help you discover more about their collections. http://images.wellcome.ac.uk

**LLOYD LIBRARY AND MUSEUM, CINCINNATI, OH**
Founded by nineteenth-century pharmacists with an interest in botany and natural herbal remedies, resources here range from 1493 to the present and cover natural history, pharmacy, medicine, and botany. Online exhibitions highlight collections. www.lloydlibrary.org

## MAPS AND CARTOGRAPHY

**OLD MAPS ONLINE (DIGITAL ONLY)**
This is a collaborative project to share early maps, developed by the Great Britain Historical GIS Project at the University of Portsmouth, UK, and Klokan Technologies, GmbH, of Switzerland. http://project.oldmapsonline.org/about

**OSHER MAP LIBRARY, UNIVERSITY OF SOUTHERN MAINE, PORTLAND, ME**
This library presents exhibitions, digitized content, and historical details on a number of cartographical themes. http://usm.maine.edu/maps/exhibitions

**LIBRARY OF CONGRESS, WASHINGTON, DC**
The Discovery and Exploration Collection invites you to browse and study the library's holdings related to maps, cartography, and geography. www.loc.gov/collection/discovery-and-exploration/about-this-collection

**MAP HISTORY (DIGITAL ONLY)**
This site acts as a gateway to online map sources that you might not have discovered otherwise, on hundreds of topics. http://maphistory.info/webimages.html

## QUILTS

**INTERNATIONAL QUILT STUDY CENTER AND MUSEUM, LINCOLN, NE**
This University of Nebraska–based research institution is the largest publicly held quilt collection in the world, and at its online Collection Explorer you can view more than a thousand quilts, see a quilt timeline, and make your own virtual quilt with swatches of historical fabrics. http://explorer.quiltstudy.org

**NATIONAL MUSEUM OF AMERICAN HISTORY, SMITHSONIAN INSTITUTION, WASHINGTON, DC**
The Smithsonian's National Quilt Collection has its roots in the nineteenth-century, and it now includes five hundred mostly American quilts from a variety of traditions. A portion of the collection can be seen online. http://americanhistory.si.edu/collections/object-groups/national-quilt-collection

## KNITTING

**WINCHESTER SCHOOL OF ART, UNIVERSITY OF SOUTHAMPTON, SOUTHAMPTON, UK**
The Richard Rutt Collection offers digitized editions of a variety of historical knitting publications and reference works related to knitting. www.southampton.ac.uk/intheloop/knittingreferencelibrary.html

**VICTORIA AND ALBERT MUSEUM, LONDON, UK**
This design museum maintains a Web page devoted to knitting, with patterns, opportunities to share projects, and ways to explore knitting materials in the museum's collections. www.vam.ac.uk/page/k/knitting/

## LETTERING, PENMANSHIP, AND TYPOGRAPHY

**WEINBERG MEMORIAL LIBRARY, UNIVERSITY OF SCRANTON, SCRANTON, PA**
Parts of the Zaner-Bloser Penmanship Collection—both printed materials as well as samples of ornamental penmanship—have been digitized and can be viewed online. http://matrix.scranton.edu/academics/wml/spcollections/z-bloser/index.shtml

**UNIVERSITY OF TEXAS AT AUSTIN, AUSTIN, TX**
The Rob Roy Kelly American Wood Type Collection, with its visual survey of the variety of wood type designs once in vogue, can be explored online. www.utexas.edu/cofa/rrk/index.php

### WALLACE CENTER, ROCHESTER INSTITUTE OF TECHNOLOGY, ROCHESTER, NY

The Cary Graphic Arts Collection contains a wealth of historical resources related to the history of graphic communication, including printers' manuals and type specimen books. They present a selection of materials online as well. http://library.rit.edu/cary

### FREE LIBRARY OF PHILADELPHIA, PHILADELPHIA, PA

Over a thousand examples of Pennsylvania German manuscript folk art and lettering called Fraktur have been digitized and can be searched and viewed online. Highlights include hand-colored birth and baptismal certificates, each embellished with bright images of birds, plants, and flowers. http://libwww.freelibrary.org/fraktur

### SAN FRANCISCO PUBLIC LIBRARY, SAN FRANCISCO, CA

The Richard Harrison Collection of Calligraphy and Lettering contains more than a thousand examples of calligraphy, extending from modern works back to medieval manuscript leaves, and it includes reference works to support the study of lettering. http://sfpl.org/index.php?pg=2000007501

### NEWBERRY LIBRARY, CHICAGO, IL

John M. Wing Foundation on the History of Printing Collection offers books, archives, and artifacts that document early typefaces and lettering styles, explore printing history, and survey technical matters related to historical printing and publishing. www.newberry.org/printing-history-and-book-arts-john-m-wing-foundation-history-printing-collection-description

## PERFORMING ARTS AND FILM

### NEW YORK PUBLIC LIBRARY FOR THE PERFORMING ARTS, NEW YORK, NY

This trove of materials related to the performing arts includes recordings, videotapes, artists' manuscripts, correspondence, sheet music, stage designs, press clippings, programs, posters and photographs. www.nypl.org/locations/lpa

### ROCK AND ROLL HALL OF FAME LIBRARY AND ARCHIVES, CLEVELAND, OH

In association with the Rock and Roll Hall of Fame, this institution's holdings include archival collections, reference sources, ephemera, and other materials that document the history of rock and roll. If you want to study Les Paul's papers, this is the place. http://library.rockhall.com/content.php?pid=290460&sid=2385875

### THE PALEY CENTER FOR MEDIA, NEW YORK, NY, AND LOS ANGELES, CA

This institution's permanent media collection includes nearly 150,000 television and radio programs as well as moving image advertisements. These can be accessed at both the New York and the Los Angeles locations. www.paleycenter.org/collection

### FREE LIBRARY OF PHILADELPHIA, PHILADELPHIA, PA

The Theatre Collection explores Philadelphia's performing arts history through print and archival collections. It includes playbills, production files, and archives of pioneer filmmakers. http://libwww.freelibrary.org/rarebooks/coll_theatre.cfm

# A COPYRIGHT PRIMER

*Librarians are often asked questions about copyright* by library users who want to make sure that they stay on the right side of the law. As a result, I've learned a little bit about what is, in truth, a pretty complicated subject. And it makes sense to share some basic information here, so that as creative users of library materials, you can feel comfortable about copyright, too.

First, some very good news: If you are making projects at home for your own personal use, you can relax. Go ahead and knit a baby sweater for your niece using that 1937 pattern you found at the library. Don't hesitate to use reproductions of newspaper headlines from the paper issued on your dad's birth date to make a decoupaged frame for him. Make a photocopy montage of images from your son's favorite illustrated books to create a custom-made coloring book just for him. Study the stitch patterns adorning an embroidered blouse in a 1950s needlework magazine you found in the library, and re-create it for your own wardrobe. If you're simply drawing inspiration or images from library resources of any kind for your own private creations, you won't generally run into problems. After all, most rights holders have better things to do than to send you a letter about how you incorporated their work into your personal project.

Legal questions can arise, however, when it comes to using other creators' published works in projects you wish to sell, publish, or exhibit. This is because your ability to freely use a source can depend in part on whether that source is or is not in what's called the public domain.

## PUBLIC DOMAIN

When a book or other resource has entered the public domain, it means that the material is free to be used, reused, adapted, mashed up, remixed, collaged, reinterpreted, and added to the mix of what you do as an artist or designer. Public domain status of works encourages creativity and new ideas.

For materials first published in the United States prior to 1923, the rule is simple—these materials are in the public domain. What does this mean? Basically, pre-1923 publications in the United States are yours to reproduce or incorporate into your own creations as you wish. That inspiration is free for the taking. So, if you want to reproduce a fabric design from an eighteenth-century pattern, re-create amazing century-old pop-up valentines, make new prints of woodcut illustrations found in an 1840s children's primer, or re-create a stunning design for a heron-embellished room divider you found in a nineteenth-century woman's magazine, you are free to do it.

Many of the projects in this book are inspired by materials that are in the public domain. Sarah Goldschadt's tiny paper house project is drawn from a 1910 issue of a children's magazine. Jodi Kahn selected an early nineteenth-century American marbled paper to print onto fabric to make her zippered pouch. And my cuts of meat embroideries take their inspiration from early twentieth-century cookbook illustrations.

Here's more good news about public domain: If the United States Government Printing Office published it, no matter when, it is also in the public domain. And while you might not think government publications could be particularly visually inspiring, remember that they released the beautiful posters that inspired my own radish love stencil pattern. The government's offerings might surprise you.

Things get more complicated for materials published in 1923 and after. Peter Hirtle, a copyright expert and Cornell University Library's senior policy advisor, has called the work of determining if something has entered the public domain to be "an uncertain art rather than a concrete science," and it can indeed be a complex affair. While you might not wish to become an expert in the ins and outs of copyright, it's a good idea to understand the basics if your commercial, exhibited, or published work incorporates post-1922 works by others. A first step in finding out what's permitted is to determine if the material is protected under copyright or if it has entered the public domain. Whether or not a work is in the public domain is determined by a number of factors, and you can start to investigate a work's copyright status by gathering answers to questions like these:

- Is the material published or unpublished?
- When was it created or published?
- Was it created or published in the United States or a different country?
- If the author or creator is no longer living, when did he or she die?
- Does the work include a copyright statement (often indicated on the verso of the title page, with a © followed by the copyright holder's name)?

With answers to these questions in hand, you are ready to consult the online resources recommended below to determine the copyright status of the work in question, or to learn more about copyright and public domain issues generally.

But even if you determine that the material you want to use is not in the public domain, that doesn't mean it's off-limits. You might decide to track down and reach out to the copyright holder to ask for permission to use their materials. When Natalie Chanin decided to include part of a contemporary poet's work on her stenciled and embroidered throw, for example, we asked and received permission from the university press that published the work, so that she could do so.

You might also consider if your proposed use of the materials could be defined as "fair use."

## FAIR USE

The "fair use" clause in U.S. copyright law permits some reuse of material under copyright, without the need to obtain permission from the copyright holder. What this means is that there may be times when you could incorporate copyrighted work into your own, without having to ask first. Whether your use is "fair" is tied to a number of issues, including: what you create, what source you use and how much of it, whether or not your work is commercial, and if your creation impacts the copyright holder's potential income. For example, I considered each of these factors before deciding to include an image of a full page of *Animals in Watermarks* in this book.

The Copyright Advisory Network site (see page 58) includes a helpful guide to determining and documenting fair use in individual cases.

## USING LIBRARIES' DIGITIZED MATERIALS

What about using all of the wonderful digitized resources that libraries share on their sites—the postcard collections, early book illustrations, photographs, archival collections, and more? Are you free to grab and use these digital images for your own purposes?

As with other materials, if you're simply using these materials for personal projects that won't be published, sold, or exhibited, then you're free to make use of these sources. But if you plan to use a library's digital sources for commercial products, exhibition, or publication, then the answer may vary from institution to institution and even from individual item to item. Some libraries freely give away high-quality digital images of everything in the public domain without restriction. Other libraries, in contrast, offer low-resolution scans at no cost but run a fee-based delivery service for those who need high-resolution versions. The British Library's Bindings Database, for example, which Ann Martin consulted when designing her quilled paper pendant, allows users to browse and study low-resolution images freely, but if you wish to use a high-resolution version for publication, you pay the library a small fee to do so.

The most secure approach, when you'd like to use library materials in commercial projects, publications, and exhibitions, is to learn what the policies are at the particular institution that interests you. This may be as easy as reading the fine print on whatever library collection site you're using—look for links called "copyright," "legal," "permissions," "reproductions," "rights information," or even just "about." If you've found their policy information and you're still not sure what it means, just write to that library to find out for certain.

## LEGAL AID

If your commercial creative work involves the active use of material that is or may be copyrighted, and if you want to be sure that your own original work is protected as well, it's worth becoming really familiar with the ins and outs of copyright. Talking with a lawyer can help.

Call your state's Bar Association to ask if there's a system or organization offering legal guidance to artists and arts organizations. And if your town has an arts center or arts organization, ask there for any ideas. If you live in the New York area, Volunteer Lawyers for the Arts (www.vlany.org) offers legal aid and continuing education programming on a variety of legal topics, including copyright.

And remember, of course, that this librarian's advice can never replace the wise counsel of a professional legal advisor.

## SOURCES FOR LEARNING MORE

**Copyright Advisory Network**
Created and maintained by the American Library Association's Office for Information Technology Policy, this site provides clear tools to learn about issues of copyright, public domain, and fair use. It also offers some easy-to-use tools for you to determine the status of a particular work, like the Public Domain Slider, the Copyright Genie, and the Fair Use Evaluator. http://librarycopyright.net

### Copyright Term and the Public Domain in the United States

Created by Cornell University Library's senior policy advisor, Peter Hirtle, this guide includes sections detailing when published and unpublished materials enter the public domain. It also addresses special cases of copyright for some special formats, including architecture and sound recordings. http://copyright.cornell.edu/resources/publicdomain.cfm

### The United States Copyright Office

This resource provides a number of useful informational pages as well as an online searchable catalog of copyright registrations from 1978 to the present. The office also maintains a paper card file of 45 million cards recording copyright registrations from 1870 to the present, which can be visited in person at the Library of Congress. www.copyright.gov

### U.S. Copyright Office Circular 22: How to Investigate the Copyright Status of a Work

One of many helpful guides posted on the site, this one introduces the steps to take when searching for a work's copyright status. www.copyright.gov/circs/circ22.pdf

### Creative Commons

This nonprofit creates free licensing tools, each built on a foundation of copyright law, that work to balance traditional "all rights reserved" copyright law with a growing interest in creative innovation online. Each license allows creators to protect their copyright while also encouraging others to make use of their work, under terms of the creator's choosing. Visit the Creative Commons site to learn about what the different licenses mean, how you can apply them to your work, and how to search for the millions of works—from documents to songs and images—that have been shared under Creative Commons licenses. http://creativecommons.org

Diagonal Spaces

Diagonal Lines

COUNTERCHANGE

58

59

PART TWO

# PROJECTS INSPIRED BY THE LIBRARY

Nina
03630076F

# Marbled Fabric Pouch

## DESIGNED BY JODI KAHN

ABOUT THE ARTIST

Jodi Kahn is a writer, crafter, and designer of accessories and home goods. She is the author of *The Little Pink Book of Elegance: The Modern Girl's Guide to Living with Style*, *Simply Sublime Bags: 30 No-Sew, Low-Sew Projects*, and *Simply Sublime Gifts: High-Style, Low-Sew Projects to Make in a Snap*. Her work has also appeared in *Real Simple*, *Country Living*, *Parade*, and other magazines. She lives in Larchmont, New York, with her family, and you'll find her online at *www.JodiKahn.com*.

Jodi's creative work often involves taking a design element or pattern out of its familiar context and applying it in a novel way. So I wasn't surprised when, as we discussed possible directions her research and project might take, she told me she wanted to reimagine historical marbled paper patterns on textiles.

She selected an early nineteenth-century specimen of marbled paper decorated in a Gloucester pattern, from a collection of marbled endpapers at the New York Public Library, as the foundation for her design. She printed the swirls of fuchsia, gold, black, and green of this historical paper on fabric sheets and turned the fabric into a booklover's travel pouch.

When I saw Jodi's design, I immediately pictured it as a grown-up pencil case of sorts, perfect for keeping pencils and erasers and other little supplies at hand when coming to the library to read, sketch, and take notes. You could just as easily use it to hold sewing notions or makeup, and its lamination provides a bit of heft as well as surface protection.

BEYOND THIS PROJECT:

This printed fabric bag provides a glimpse of the possibilities for using marbled and other decorated and patterned papers as quickly applied design elements. Because the fabric printed with these patterns is made in 8½ × 11" (22 × 28cm) sheets, it's ideal for all kinds of small stitching projects, like an eReader cover or a set of laminated coasters. You might also combine a variety of marbled sheets to create a book tote or a patchwork quilt.

Jodi's method of printing marbled patterns on fabric is quick and satisfying. But if you are mesmerized by marbling and want to learn more about its history, browse historical and modern samples of decorated papers, and maybe even learn to make your own, check out the sources on page 69.

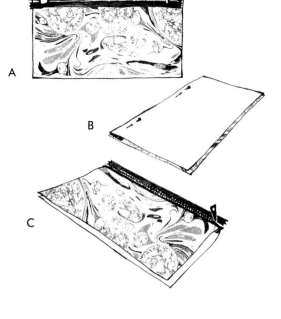

A

B

C

FINISHED DIMENSIONS

- 2" (5cm) deep × 7" (18cm) long × 3½" (9cm) tall

SUPPLIES

- Two 8½ × 11" (22 × 28cm) printable fabric sheets
- Scan or digital image of marbled paper of your own choosing*, or download the Gloucester Marble pattern (from http://handmadelibrarian.com/marbledpaper)
- Two 8½ × 11" (22 × 28cm) pieces iron-on vinyl
- 9" (23cm) zipper
- ¼ yard (23cm) broadcloth for lining the bag, in color of your choice
- Sewing machine equipped with zipper foot
- Thread to match fabric
- Iron and ironing board
- 2" (5cm) tassel for zipper pull

*If you choose a marbled paper from a library's digital collection, you may wish to check with the library about their policies on the use of digitized images, because some contemporary decorated papers may be protected by copyright or have other rights restrictions. For more information on copyright, see page 55.

## STEP 1. PREPARE MARBLED PAPER–PATTERNED FABRIC

Following instructions on package of printable fabric sheets, print two fabric sheets with marbled-paper scan, digital image, or Gloucester Marble pattern.

Following instructions on package of iron-on vinyl, laminate right side (printed side) of each printed fabric sheet.

## STEP 2. CUT FABRICS

Cut two 5 × 10½" (13 × 27cm) rectangles from laminated printed fabric sheets and two 5 × 10½" (13 × 27cm) rectangles from broadcloth lining fabric.

## STEP 3. SEW ZIPPER IN PLACE

Place a printed fabric rectangle right side up on work surface. Place closed zipper on top, face down, so one of zipper's fabric edges is centered along one long edge of marbled rectangle (illustration A).Top this with a rectangle of broadcloth lining fabric, right side down, and pin all three layers together along long edge (illustration B). The zipper will be hidden in between fabric layers, with its one edge lined up right between long edges of two fabrics.

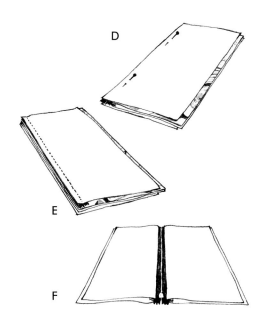

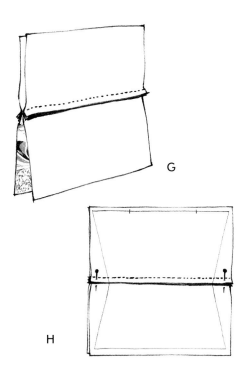

Using zipper foot on sewing machine, sew the three layers together along the long pinned edge, using a ¼" (5mm) seam allowance.

Open up the two layers of fabric and fold them back so wrong sides are together and zipper's teeth and unstitched fabric edge stand out from sewn layers (illustration C). Applying iron only to lining side, iron fabric layers away from zipper.

Attach other side of zipper to remaining printed fabric and broadcloth lining rectangles: Place printed fabric rectangle right side up, then lay free fabric edge of zipper face down on top, so it is centered along and lines up evenly with long edge of marbled rectangle underneath it. Top this with second rectangle of broadcloth lining fabric, right side down, and pin all three layers together (illustration D).

Using zipper foot on sewing machine, sew the three layers together along the long pinned edge, using a ¼" (5mm) seam allowance (illustration E).

As with the first side, open up these two layers of fabric, fold them back so wrong sides are together, and iron only

lining side so fabric layers are pressed away from zipper (illustration F).

### STEP 4. CREATE BASIC BAG SHAPE
Turn over sewn fabric and zipper so printed side faces up. Open zipper 6" (15cm).

Open fabric layers so right sides of printed fabrics face each other and right sides of broadcloth lining pieces also face each other (illustration G).

Draw shape of bag: Measure in 1½" (4cm) from each side along zipper seam. Mark each of these points with pencil. Next, draw a diagonal line from each 1½" (4cm) mark to bottom and top corners of bag, then measure ¼" (5mm) in from each of long edges and draw a line straight across (illustration H).

Switch to machine's regular foot and stitch along pencil line, starting about 2" (5cm) from corner of broadcloth lining side's long edge.

Stitch around bag, sewing over zipper teeth, stopping about 6" (15cm) before you reach starting point to leave an unstitched opening along long edge of lining. Trim all seam allowances, except for unstitched opening along long edge of lining, to ¼" (5mm) (illustration I).

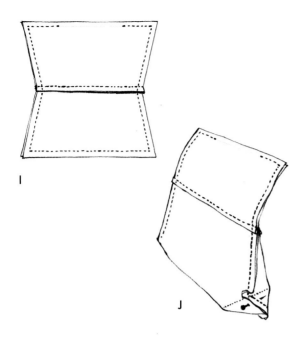

I

J

## STEP 5. SEW CORNER GUSSETS

Reach into case through zipper opening
and pinch each corner together so side
seam and bottom seam line up. Pin in
place. Repeat so all four corners are
pinned this way (illustration J).

Sew across each corner, 1½" (4cm)
away from bottom point. (Note: Corner
seam will measure approximately 2" [5cm]
across.) Clip four corners ¼" (5mm) away
from seam.

## STEP 6. COMPLETE BAG

Turn bag right side out through open
zipper. Before tucking lining inside,
fold raw edges of unstitched opening to
wrong side and press folded raw edges
together. Machine-sew this opening
closed.

Iron lining side of bag, and tuck it
inside marbled fabric side of bag.

To press any wrinkles out of marbled
side of bag, make sure to place protective
sheet from laminating paper or a piece of
parchment paper on top of marbled fabric.
*Do not* iron directly on marbled fabric or
laminated protective coating may melt.

Thread tassel's top loop through hole
in zipper pull, draw tassel through loop,
and cinch gently to secure.

RIGHT Marbled papers have been made by hand for
a thousand years and can be found in a wide variety of
patterns and colors. This example dates from the early
nineteenth century.

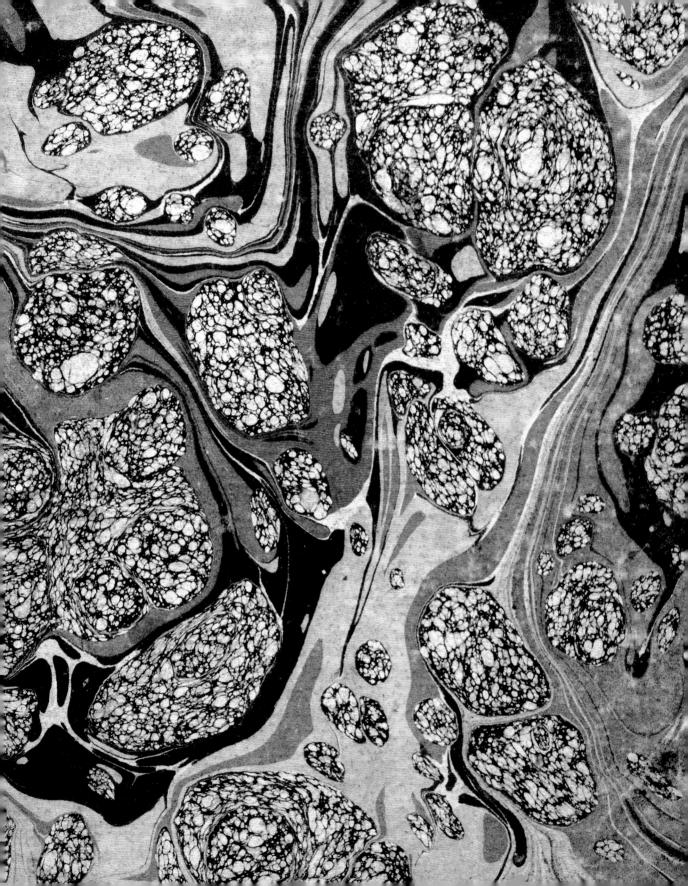

# DECORATED PAPERS

A book's endpapers, or endleaves—folded double leaves of paper, with the back side of one half pasted down to the inside cover of a book and the other half remaining free—are the first thing you see when you peek inside a volume's front cover. Long ago, bookbinders added luxury and elegance to their work by using beautifully hand-decorated papers. In books today, endpapers may be less flamboyantly adorned than in the eighteenth century, but it's always a treat to find a modern book with a handy map, a family tree, or an unexpected pattern printed there.

Marbled papers made their way from Asia to Europe via trade routes through Italy, and by the eighteenth century, these hand-decorated papers became the endpapers of choice in books throughout much of Europe. Marbled paper, though perhaps the most recognizable, is not the only form of decorated paper used as endpapers in books. Paste paper is created by making textural patterns in a mixture of thinned paste and pigment spread across a sheet of paper. You also might encounter Dutch gilt papers, which feature metallic patterns, and stenciled papers.

Because decorated papers are tied directly to the history of book arts and bookbinding, research libraries will often have examples in their collections.

Here are a few recommended library collections:

> The Rosamond B. Loring Collection of Decorated Papers (*52L-1000). Houghton Library, Harvard University. Approximately 10,000 pieces of decorated paper dating from the sixteenth to the twentieth century.

> Decorated and Decorative Papers (Digital Collections, University of Washington): http://content.lib.washington.edu/dpweb

Want to search at your library for more on marbled and other decorated papers? Here are some Subject Headings to use in your catalog search:

> COLORED PAPERS — SPECIMENS.
> DECORATIVE PAPER — SPECIMENS.
> MARBLED PAPERS — HISTORY.
> MARBLED PAPERS — SPECIMENS.
> MARBLING (BOOKBINDING).
> PAPER, HANDMADE.
> PASTE PAPERS — SPECIMENS.

I recommend the following sources for learning about the history of decorated papers and techniques for making your own:

> *The Art of Marbled Paper: Marbled Patterns and How to Make Them.* Miura Einen. New York: Kodansha International, 1990.

> *Marbled Paper: Its History, Techniques, and Patterns: With Special Reference to the Relationship of Marbling to Bookbinding in Europe and the Western World.* Richard J. Wolfe. Philadelphia: University of Pennsylvania Press, 1990.

> *Decorated Book Papers: Being an Account of their Designs and Fashions.* Rosamond B. Loring. Cambridge, Massachusetts: Department of Printing and Graphic Arts, Harvard College Library, 1942.

> *Paper Pleasures: The Creative Guide to Papercraft.* Faith Shannon. New York: Weidenfeld and Nicolson in association with Il Papiro, 1987.

LEFT This marbled paper forms the endleaves of Voltaire's eighteenth-century bound manuscript of *La Pucelle d'Orleans.*

# Watermark Pillows

## DESIGNED BY JESSICA PIGZA

The earliest papermakers in Europe made paper by hand, one sheet at a time, using a wood-and-wire frame called a mould. Many papermakers incorporated subtle designs in their moulds with a length of bent and shaped wire, and these designs acted as brands to identify the maker or mill that had made that particular sheet of paper. These designs, known as watermarks, revealed themselves when a light was shined through a sheet of handmade paper. The watermarks appeared as a light variance in the texture of the paper.

Watermarks can be found in the shape of animals like dogs and oxen and lions, fantastical creatures like unicorns and mermaids, and even everyday items like scissors and knives. Because watermark designs are the result of bending wires into a flat pictorial shape, they often look like quirky line drawings, ready to be adapted as embroidery designs.

On these pillows, I enlarged two watermarks to exploit their graphic possibilities. The whale watermark was used by the mill of Dutch papermaker Adriaan Rogge, and the rooster was found on a sheet of fifteenth-century paper associated with the Spanish city of Orihuela. Both of these designs are recorded in *Animals in Watermarks* by Francisco de Bofarull y Sans.

BEYOND THIS PROJECT:

These designs can provide craft inspiration for any number of surface design projects and embellishments and can be applied to a variety of embroidery and paper projects, at different sizes. They can be used to embellish a T-shirt, or to add a hand-embroidered border along the hemline of a skirt. They can be added to cloth napkins and tablecloths, or embroidered onto individual squares and sewn into a patchwork quilt.

And because each watermark has a history, you can select watermark designs that are meaningful to you. If you're making a gift for friends who will be honeymooning in France, for instance, you could choose watermark designs from that country.

Use the suggested sources on page 74 to discover more watermark designs for your own creative work.

## FINISHED DIMENSIONS

WHALE: 15½ × 11" (39 × 28cm)

ROOSTER: 17 × 17" (43 × 43cm)

## SUPPLIES

### FOR WHALE

- Two 16½ × 12" (42 × 30cm) pieces light blue wool felt
- One 25-meter skein of crewel wool in gray

### FOR ROOSTER

- Two 18" (46cm) squares pale yellow-green wool felt
- One 25-meter skein of crewel wool in dark teal

### FOR BOTH

- Dressmaker's tracing paper
- Dull pencil, or other bluntly pointed object (a knitting needle works well)
- Straight pins
- Fine-tip permanent marker
- Embroidery hoop
- Crewel needle
- Iron and ironing board
- Sewing machine
- All-purpose thread, in colors to match felt
- Polyester fiberfill (24 ounces will be enough for both pillows)
- Hand-sewing needle

Note: The directions for making each pillow are the same. Just use the felt, crewel wool, and thread colors appropriate for each pillow.

### STEP 1: TRANSFER DESIGN TO PILLOW TOP

Photocopy design template on page 73, enlarging it 200% for the whale and 325% for the rooster. You may need to piece together the enlarged template.

Place one of the felt pieces on a the smooth surface—this will be the pillow top. Place a sheet of dressmaker's tracing paper face down on felt. Carefully center photocopied design, right side up, on top of tracing paper and felt. Secure layers with straight pins so they won't shift.

Using a dull pencil or other bluntly pointed object, trace over watermark template lines, transferring design onto felt.

After design has been transferred, remove pins and set aside tracing paper and template. Place felt right side up on a smooth surface and retrace, tracing paper lines lightly and carefully with fine-tip permanent marker.

### STEP 2: STITCH DESIGN

Place felt in embroidery hoop and tighten hoop. (If you don't finish project in one sitting, remove felt from embroidery hoop while not working on it to keep it from becoming misshapen.)

Using crewel wool and a crewel needle, embroider over pattern drawn on felt. For Whale, use chainstitch to embroider body and backstitch for spouting water. For Rooster, use chainstitch for entire design.

### STEP 3: PRESS PILLOW TOP AND BOTTOM

When embroidery is completed, remove felt from embroidery hoop. Sandwich felt, right side down, between two fluffy towels, and gently press with iron, using only slight pressure and plenty of steam. Gently press unembellished piece of felt in same way—this will be pillow bottom.

### STEP 4: CONSTRUCT PILLOW

Pin pillow top and bottom, right sides together, all around edges. Use a sewing machine and matching thread to stitch all around pillow with a $3/8$" (1cm) seam allowance, leaving an 8" (20cm) opening at center of bottom seam.

Clip corners of two sewn layers diagonally, cutting close to corner but not cutting seam. This will allow corners to easily turn right side out.

Turn pillow right side out through opening in bottom seam, making sure to turn corners out fully.

Stuff pillow with fiberfill to desired firmness, adding a small handful at a time so pillow will not be lumpy.

Use a hand-sewing needle and all-purpose thread to whipstitch opening closed.

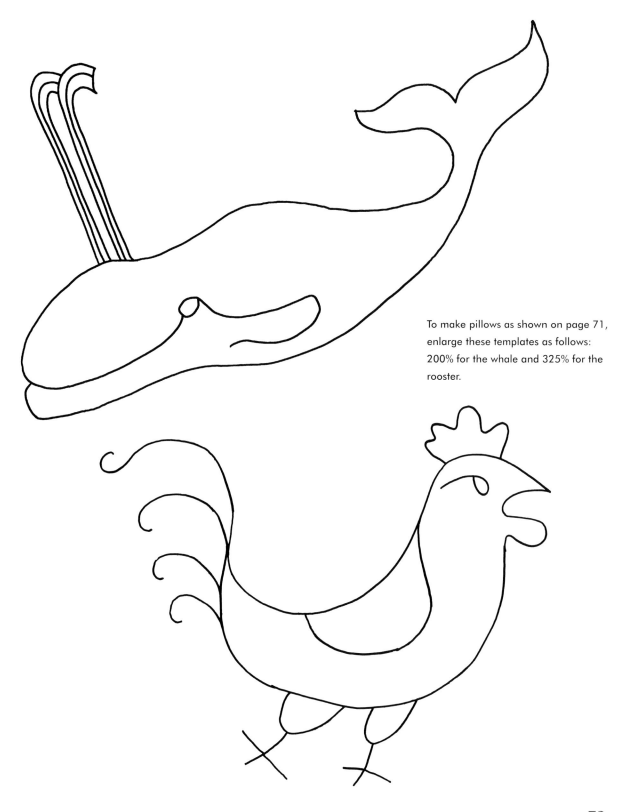

To make pillows as shown on page 71,
enlarge these templates as follows:
200% for the whale and 325% for the
rooster.

# WATERMARKS ON HANDMADE PAPER

While not every sheet of early handmade paper will have a watermark revealing the paper's origin, finding and identifying a watermark can provide a researcher with a welcome clue to where an early printed book or a handwritten letter might have begun its life hundreds of years ago. The reference sources that scholars turn to when they need to identify the origin of a particular watermark can be found both in print and online. They work like a visual directory of drawings and scans of watermarks that have been found and identified by previous scholars.

For crafters and designers, these reference sources provide inspiration in the form of hundreds of watermarks gathered in a single place, often organized by what the watermark represents (at right is a glimpse of what one guide to watermarks looks like, with a variety of bird watermarks all presented together). There are a number of excellent works that document and reproduce watermarks from handmade papers of past centuries. Here are a few:

*Animals in Watermarks*. Francisco de Bofarull y Sans. Hilversum, Holland: Paper Publications Society, 1959.

*Les Filigranes: Dictionnaire Historique des Marques du Papier dès leur Apparition vers 1282 jusqu'en 1600*. C. M. Briquet. Amsterdam: Paper Publications Society (Labarre Foundation), 1968.

Watermarks of the Middle Ages (Austrian Academy of Sciences): www.ksbm.oeaw.ac.at/wz

Piccard Watermark Collection (Hauptstaatsarchiv Stuttgart): www.piccard-online.de

The Thomas L. Gravell Watermark Archive (the University of Delaware Library and the Bibliothèe de Genève): www.gravell.org

Watermark Database of the Dutch University Institute for Art History: www.wm-portal.net/niki

Watermarks in Incunabula Printed in the Low Countries (National Library of the Netherlands): http://watermark.kb.nl

You'll be able to find more sources on papermaking at your library by using these Subject Headings:

PAPER, HANDMADE — HISTORY.
PAPERMAKING — HISTORY.
WATERMARKS.
WATERMARKS — BIBLIOGRAPHIES.
WATERMARKS — INDEXES.

RIGHT *Animals in Watermarks*, which is organized by type of animal, held the inspirational rooster I used on my watermark pillow.

514

515

516

518

517

521

# Ornamental Penmanship Embroidery

## DESIGNED BY MARY CORBET

ABOUT THE ARTIST
Mary Corbet is a needlework artist and teacher who offers needlework instruction, including children's embroidery classes, both in person and online. She is also an avid collector of needlework books. Mary lives in northeast Kansas. You'll find her online at her popular needlework blog, needlenthread.com, where she shares histories of needlework, reviews books, offers tutorials, and reports on her own projects.

Calligraphy, illumination, handwriting, penmanship—embroidery artist Mary Corbet has long been interested in these pursuits because lettering styles often mirror embroideries from the same time period and place. The fine English embroidery of the thirteenth century known as opus anglicanum, for example, presents the same densely colored fields and frameworks as illuminated manuscripts of the same era. And in Victorian England, monograms appeared on textiles as whitework. And of course, the alphabet itself is a perennial presence on samplers.

While gathering ideas for her ornamental penmanship–inspired embroidery pattern, Mary turned to early printed books like George Bickham's *The Universal Penman*, and she also browsed through penmanship exercises in the Horace Grant Healey Penmanship Collection at the New York Public Library.

In creating her bird design, Mary faced the challenge of interpreting a very flat design as an intricate three-dimensional work, with layers of thread and closely worked lines. She found that by simplifying her design in subtle ways, she could preserve the flourishing lines while also making a workable embroidery pattern. When deciding on color, Mary experimented with multiple colors and even gold thread before deciding to take a lesson from the ornamental penmanship itself, which uses just a single color of ink in lines of varying width. Her redwork bird uses just one color and one stitch (stem stitch), except for the bird's eye, which is satin stitch. Her design, applied to a vintage-style linen tea towel, nods to the past while remaining bright and fresh.

BEYOND THIS PROJECT:

Mary's redwork bird design can be interpreted using a variety of embroidery techniques. It would translate well into whitework embroidery or as surface embroidery with a variety of stitches. You can adapt the design to your skill level and interests, and it can also be enlarged to embellish a large area, such as an apron or a summer skirt.

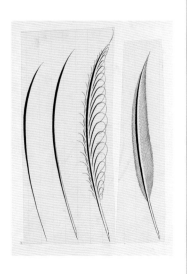

These feathers were created by students during the Golden Age of American penmanship.

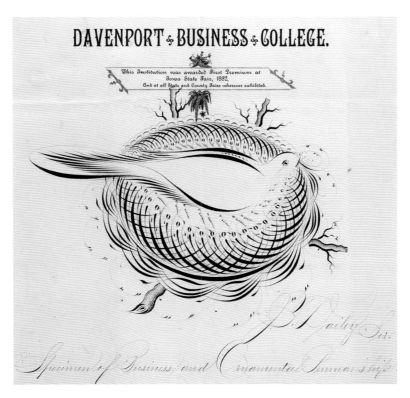

This bird's nest is a sample of students' ornamental penmanship in the nineteenth century.

## FINISHED DIMENSIONS

- Embroidery measures 7½ × 4" (19 × 10cm)

## SUPPLIES

- White linen or cotton tea towel
- Iron and ironing board
- Spray starch
- Tape
- Straight pins
- Pencil
- 4 or 5" (10 or 13cm) embroidery hoop
- One skein cotton floche (same as coton a broder) in red (unlike some embroidery threads, cotton floche is used in a single strand and should never be divided further into thinner strands)
- #9 crewel needle
- Small, sharp scissors

### STEP 1. PREPARE FABRIC

Wash linen or cotton towel before stitching on it, to remove sizing and minimize shrinkage when laundering later.

Iron towel with spray starch until smooth and wrinkle-free.

### STEP 2. TRANSFER DESIGN

Photocopy pattern on page 79, enlarging it by 150% so that it is approximately 7½" (19cm) wide at its widest point.

Tape pattern to a light box or a sunny window. Situate towel over design, aligning it to where you want design to end up. Using sewing pins, carefully pin towel to design, just outside design area. Slide pins into paper at an angle, but do not bring tip of pin back out onto fabric or paper. Pin towel at all four corners, then pin between those four pins, so that fabric is held in place.

Using pencil, trace design onto fabric. Trace in long, smooth lines rather than short, sketchy lines.

To make this embroidery as shown on page 77, enlarge the template by 150%.

## STEP 3. EMBROIDER BIRD

Place towel in embroidery hoop so left half of bird is in hoop, positioning it so as much of design as possible will fit (you can move hoop around as needed while stitching). Fabric should be drum-tight in the hoop.

Using a strand of cotton floche and a #9 crewel needle, work stem stitch over all thin lines of design. Then, referring to pattern, go back and fill all solid areas in diagram with more lines of closely worked stem stitch.

Satin-stitch bird's eye.

## STEP 4. FINISH TOWEL

Rinse tea towel in cold water and lay it flat on a bath towel. Roll up bath towel and gently squeeze out all excess water.

Allow embroidered towel to dry most of the way.

While still slightly damp, place towel, embroidery side down, on a well-padded, smooth, soft ironing board. Iron towel on back side with a hot, dry iron until smooth and free of wrinkles. Do not iron to dry tea towel, but rather to remove wrinkles.

When surface is smooth and wrinkle-free, lay embroidered tea towel on a flat surface to finish drying.

# CALLIGRAPHY AND PENMANSHIP

If you're interested in letterforms and handwriting history, the possibilities for study and design inspiration in the library are countless. Perhaps, like embroidery artist Mary Corbet, you are fascinated by ornamental penmanship's potential for interpretation in stitches. This style of handwriting is well known for its looping flourishes depicting everything from human profiles to cherubs, fish to birds. Ornamental penmanship is now famously associated with the golden age of American penmanship in the nineteenth century, when those possessing elegant, consistent handwriting became invaluable employees in business offices where typewriters weren't yet everyday equipment.

Elaborate styles of penmanship and engrossing (adding flourishing, decorative embellishments to handwritten documents) have a much longer history than just nineteenth-century America, however. Research libraries contain a variety of printed works from earlier centuries offering specimens of ornate alphabets, frames, borders, and more. Johann Georg Schwandner's *Calligraphia Latina* (1756), John Seddon's *The Pen-mans Paradis* (1695), and George Bickham's *The Universal Penman* (1733) are a few examples.

The ornamental and graphically bold designs displayed in examples of ornamental penmanship can be used in both small and large scale for linear embroidery designs. You might also draw on these sources to create a personal monogram, a card or letterhead design, a tattoo, a stamp, or just about any other surface design.

The following collections offer a wealth of source material on penmanship:

The Zaner-Bloser Penmanship Collection at Weinberg Memorial Library (University of Scranton) is an exceptional source of printed and manuscript materials. Portions available online at digitalservices.scranton.edu/cdm/landingpage/collection/zanerbloser.

The International Association of Master Penman, Engrossers, and Teachers of Handwriting (IAMPETH) offers digitized books and periodicals highlighting America's golden age of penmanship in their online library at www.iampeth.com.

The Horace Grant Healey Penmanship Collection at the New York Public Library (Manuscripts and Archives Division) contains a wealth of examples of penmanship by teacher Horace Grant Healey and exercises by his penmanship students as well. Although it has not been digitized, this collection can be studied if you visit the library in person.

These Subject Headings will help you in your search for more library sources on penmanship and handwriting:

CALLIGRAPHY.

COMMERCIAL CORRESPONDENCE — EARLY WORKS TO 1800.

COPYBOOKS.

PENMANSHIP — SPECIMENS.

WRITING — SPECIMENS.

WRITING — SYSTEMS.

Books like *The Pen-mans Paradis* (detail above) and *The Universal Penman* (detail right) reveal the long history of calligraphy and ornamental penmanship in England.

# Secret Message Snowflakes and Patterned Stationery Set

## DESIGNED BY JULIE SCHNEIDER

ABOUT THE ARTIST
Julie Schneider is the community manager at Etsy, where she develops educational content for sellers and organizes hands-on workshops. A Brooklyn resident, she also creates and sells handmade books, art, and paper goods for her own shop, Your Secret Admiral (www.etsy.com/shop/yoursecretadmiral) and teaches craft classes.

Artist Julie Schneider often uses cut paper as her medium to create cards, home décor, and other paper goods. But she also loves letterpress, and she sought inspiration for her projects in a variety of type specimen books at the New York Public Library. The results of her study are two type-inspired designs—a secret message snowflake and a patterned stationery set—that both make use of familiar letters in unexpected and even abstract ways.

She selected the two letters she features in her projects, $U$ and $I$, from an 1892 wood type specimen book published by the Hamilton Manufacturing Company of Two Rivers, Wisconsin. Julie was especially drawn to the examples of wood type because she appreciated how the unique irregularities of stamped or cut paper are similar to the scratches and wear that wood type gathers over time.

BEYOND THESE PROJECTS:

The secret message snowflakes could be easily transformed into decorations for Valentine's Day by using red and pink papers and incorporating small heart cutouts into your design. And you can create your own monogrammed stationery by creating stamps of your initial letters that you find in type specimen books. You might also find a boldly scaled letter or ornament that would be perfect as a stencil for decorating textiles. See page 88 for ideas on where to find and browse wood type specimen books on your own.

RIGHT: In her research, Julie was drawn to bold letterforms like these specimens of wood type offered for sale in 1872 by William H. Page & Co. of Greeneville, Connecticut.

All Type and Borders, shown in this Book, have a name or number printed over it, by which it may be ordered, and therefore the pages need not be mutilated by cutting out specimen lines, &c. to order by.

6 Line Egyptian Ornamented.     D. 7 Cents.

# Court District
# SHORE LINE

8 Line Egyptian Ornamented.     D. 9 Cents.

# Demented
# ISTHMUS

10 Line Egyptian Ornamented.     D. 11 Cents.

# REDER

12 Line Egyptian Ornamented.     D. 13 Cents.

# LIMES

In ordering, leave out no part of the name or number printed over the line. The price for all sizes will be found in the Price List. All Letters made any size desired.

15 Line Egyptian Ornamented.     D. 16 Cents.

# ROSE

20 Line Egyptian Ornamented.     D. 19 Cents.

# SEN

25 Line Egyptian Ornamented.     D. 23 Cents.

# TN

# SECRET MESSAGE SNOWFLAKES

## FINISHED DIMENSIONS

- Approximately 7", 6", or 5" in (18cm / 15cm / 13cm) diameter

## SUPPLIES

- Craft knife
- Cutting mat
- 8½ × 11" (22 × 28cm) sheet lightweight paper (such as rice paper)
- Pencil
- Craft scissors

Note: The instructions for making the snowflakes are identical for all three sizes.

## STEP 1: CREATE TEMPLATES

The template at right is sized to make snowflakes approximately 6" (15cm) in diameter. Photocopy template, enlarging it to 120% or reducing it to 85% if desired, to make 7" or 5" (17.5 or 12.5cm) snowflakes. Using craft knife and cutting mat, cut out template along solid and dotted lines.

## STEP 2: FOLD SNOWFLAKE PAPER

Trim a sheet of lightweight paper to appropriate size for size of snowflake you wish to make: an 8" (20cm) square for large, 7" (17.5cm) square for medium, or 6" (15cm) square for small.

Fold square in half diagonally. Fold this triangle in half again, and then fold in half a third time.

## STEP 3: CUT OUT LETTERS

Using template and pencil, line up pointed end of template with point of folded paper. Referring to template diagram at right, trace solid cutting lines (not dotted lines, which are for placement guidance only) onto folded paper's top layer. Set template aside.

Working slowly and carefully with a craft knife on a cutting mat, cut out along each penciled line, cutting through all layers of folded paper. Start with U shape. Next, cut each I, first cutting out rectangle shape and then cutting out tiny points.

Use craft scissors to cut along curved line opposite point.

## STEP 4: COMPLETE SNOWFLAKE

Carefully unfold cut paper. To flatten it, you may wish to place it inside a large closed book for a day or more.

At this point, the snowflake may be used as you wish. Multiple snowflakes can be used to decorate a wall, window, or mirror. A series laid down the center of a table will make a lacy paper alternative to a table runner. You could also simply refold one partially to send in the mail as a gift, or mount it on bright paper and frame it.

This template can be reduced or enlarged to create different sizes of snowflakes.

# PATTERNED STATIONERY SET

FINISHED DIMENSIONS

- 3 × 4¾" (8 × 12cm) cards with 3½ × 4⅞" (8 × 12.5cm) envelopes

SUPPLIES

- 8½ × 11" (22 × 28cm) sheet soft white cardstock (one sheet makes two cards)
- Two 3½ × 4⅞" (8 × 12.5cm) envelopes
- Metal ruler
- Pencil
- Craft knife
- Cutting mat
- Scrap paper
- Carving block (such as E-Z-Cut or Speedy-Cut)
- Transfer paper (optional)
- Scrap cardstock
- Ink pad
- Scissors
- Corner rounder

## STEP 1: CUT CARDS
Fold sheet of cardstock in half vertically. Using metal ruler and pencil, measure and mark center point on each long edge. Connect marks to indicate center of folded cardstock, then use craft knife and cutting mat to cut two folded cards, each measuring 3 × 4¾" (8 × 12cm).

## STEP 2: MAKE STAMP
Photocopy I template at right. Make a sandwich with a carving block on bottom, transfer paper in middle (carbon side down), and I template photocopy on top. Use pencil to trace firmly over template. If you don't have transfer paper, simply shade entire back side of photocopied template with pencil. Lay template on top of carving block with shaded side down, and use a pencil to firmly trace over template lines; shading will transfer to carving block.

On a cutting mat, use a craft knife to cut all around template. Using long part of craft knife blade rather than just tip is helpful here. Resulting stamp is shaped just like the template design.

## STEP 3: DECORATE CARDS
Before stamping your card, practice stamping on scrap pieces of cardstock until you are comfortable with the inking process, the pressure used, and your desired stamp pattern. For each stamp, press stamp evenly onto stamp pad and then carefully place it on paper and apply firm, even pressure across entire stamp before lifting it off paper.

Place fresh sheet of scrap paper on your work surface, and place one of the cards from step 1 on top. Begin by placing your first stamp roughly in middle of card, and add stamps above, below, and to right and left as you work.

Allow stamped card to dry thoroughly.

## STEP 4: ROUND CORNERS
Use a corner rounder to clip each of the card's four corners.

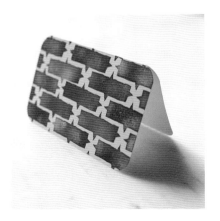
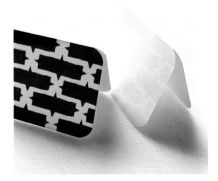
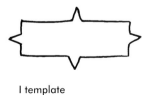

I template

# TYPE SPECIMENS

Type specimen books functioned like catalogs or sales brochures in centuries past, allowing letterpress type foundries, which produced metal or wood type, and printers an efficient means of advertising the variety of styles they had available for use or purchase. In addition to various typefaces, type specimen books also showed the variety of sizes, different alphabets, and other type ornaments one could purchase.

Looking at historical type specimen books today can provide a way to study many type designs in a single place, opening a window into the type designs common at a particular place and time in history. Even if you aren't designing type, you'll find plenty of inspiration and ideas from studying the ornaments, borders, and other decorative cuts commonly found alongside sample alphabets in specimen books.

When an early nineteenth-century woodworking innovation resulted in the ability to mass-produce display type from wood, a new letterpress aesthetic was born. Wood type—with its giant-size letters and dramatic shapes—was embraced by sign makers, poster printers, and others who needed bold, eye-catching options for their designs. And unlike specimen books for metal type, which could be quite diminutive, wood type specimen books were, by necessity, giant volumes. Their pages had to be large enough to display the sample letterforms, and they were often printed in a variety of boldly colored inks as well.

Many research libraries with an interest in the history of printing will include type specimen books for wood or metal type in their collections. Here are some collections especially worth pursuing:

Cary Graphic Arts Collection at the Wallace Center, Rochester Institute of Technology Libraries, is a growing collection of type specimen books and printers' manuals.

Rob Roy Kelly American Wood Type Collection at the University of Texas at Austin: http://www.utexas.edu/cofa/rrk/index.php

Web Museum of Wood Types and Ornaments has digitized wood type specimen books from a number of historical companies like Hamilton and Page: www.unicorngraphics.com/wood%20type%20museum.asp

Briar Press maintains an online library of cuts and caps—historical ornaments, letters, frames, borders, symbols, and other ornaments made originally for printing with letterpress type. These are fun to browse, and in many cases they are also free to use for personal projects: http://www.briarpress.org/cuts

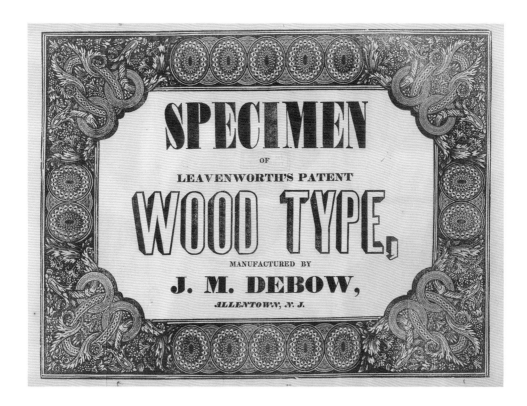

And if you'd like to read more about the history of type, check out these books:

*Alphabets to Order: The Literature of Nineteenth-Century Typefounders' Specimens.* Alistair Johnston. New Castle, Delaware: Oak Knoll Press, 2000.

*A Short History of the Printed Word.* Warren Chappell. Boston: Nonpareil, 1980.

*Typeforms: A History.* Alan Bartram. London: British Library; New Castle, Delaware: Oak Knoll, 2007.

These Subject Headings will lead to more resources at the library on type specimens and printing history:

Printing — History.
Printing — Specimens.
Type and Type-Founding.
Type and Type-Founding — Specimens.
Type — Specimens.
Wood Types.

# Quilled Willow Pendant

## DESIGNED BY ANN MARTIN

ABOUT THE ARTIST
Ann Martin, a quilling enthusiast, is the author of *All Things Paper: 20 Unique Projects from Leading Paper Crafters, Artists, and Designers* and *Creative Paper Quilling*. She explores the worlds of creative paper art and paper craft online at AllThingsPaper.net.

ABOVE: This 1898 binding, with its gilt blossoms and leaves, reveals the design potential of historical and fine book bindings.

Quilling, also known as paper filigree, has been practiced for centuries. This craft's artisans have included Renaissance-era monastic monks and nuns, skilled ladies in Victorian England, and even Jane Austen's heroine Elinor Dashwood in 1811's *Sense and Sensibility*, who contrives to assist Lucy Steele in completing a filigree basket so she can have an important conversation "without any risk of being heard at the card-table."

Quilling's past might be full of reliquaries, tea caddies, and decorated baskets, but it has made a modern comeback as stationery, paper sculpture, jewelry, ornamental lettering, and more. And because at its most basic level, quilling requires just glue, paper strips, and something to coil the strips around, it's easy to give it a try with little or no investment.

Paper filigree artist and enthusiast Ann Martin, who created this pendant, often looks to wrought-iron scrollwork, fabric patterns, and natural forms for inspiration. For this project, she turned to a selection of historic bookbindings, each decorated with patterns of branches and leaves in gold tooling. These natural-looking curving forms were an obvious choice for interpretation in paper, Ann felt, and her use of metallic-edged quilling paper adds elegance to the pendant even as it plays with the expectations of paper and metal.

BEYOND THIS PROJECT:

The willow design can also be used to create dramatic earrings that will be quite light despite their size (but are best when worn with your hair up so that it doesn't tangle in the papery branches). Just make two of the design, and attach earring wires through the jump rings. The measurements could also be divided in half to make smaller earrings, just 1" (2.5cm) in diameter, although Ann feels that working with such short strips should only be attempted after a fair amount of practice.

Looking for more bookbinding design inspiration? Turn to page 94 to find out about libraries' historic bookbinding collections that you can browse online for inspiration.

- 2" (5cm) diameter pendant

- Craft glue
- Small dish, for holding glue
- Toothpick
- Ten 17 × ⅛" (43cm × 3mm) paper quilling strips in silver-edged black
- Damp, lint-free cloth
- Scissors
- Ruler
- Quilling tool, either needle or slotted type
- Two pairs of jewelry pliers
- Jump ring, large enough to accommodate necklace chain
- Necklace chain, cording, or ribbon of your choice
- Liquitex Varnish (optional)
- Small paintbrush (optional)
- Small cup (optional)
- Adhesive tape (optional)

### STEP 1: MAKE PENDANT COIL STACK

Place a dab of glue in small dish.

Use a toothpick to apply thin, even coating of glue along entire length of one 17 × ⅛" (43cm × 3mm) quilling strip. Adhere this strip to a second strip, making sure silver edges both face same way. Apply glue along entire length of second strip and adhere third strip on top of second, again making sure silver edges face same way.

When three strips are glued together, run a damp cloth gently down both sides of stacked strips to remove any excess glue.

Set stacked strip aside until glue is completely dry.

### STEP 2: MAKE MARQUISE-SHAPED (LEAF) COILS

Cut paper quilling strips into following sizes and quantities:

Thirty 3 × ⅛" (8cm × 3mm) segments
Two 2½ × ⅛" (6cm × 3mm) segments
One 2 × ⅛" (5cm × 3mm) segment

Use a quilling tool (either needle type or slotted type) to coil each of these segments into marquise-shaped (leaf) coils.

If using a needle tool (illustration A), dampen thumb and index finger of whichever hand feels most comfortable rolling paper. Place one end of a strip across end of needle and roll paper with thumb and index finger while holding tool handle with the other hand. Be sure to rotate paper, not tool.

If using a slotted tool (illustration B), insert one end of a strip into slot, taking care that it does not extend beyond end of slot. Roll strip by turning tool with one hand and guiding paper with other.

When strip is fully rolled (illustration C) using either tool, allow coil to relax and slide it off tool. Pinch coil between your thumb and forefinger to flatten it, then pinch opposing points to form flattened coil into a marquise (leaf) shape (illustration D). Try to make all the marquises of the same strip length the same finished size.

Use a toothpick to apply a very small amount of glue to strip end and press it in place (illustration E). Trim any excess paper and gently wipe off excess glue with a damp cloth as needed.

### STEP 3: MAKE PENDANT SPIRAL

Before proceeding with this step, be sure pendant coil stack created in Step 1 is completely dry; otherwise layers will separate and buckle.

Roll pendant coil stack created in Step 1 around handle of quilling tool (illustration F).

Slip coil off tool, allow it to relax a bit, and gently shape it until spiral is approximately 2" (5cm) in diameter (illustration G). Layered strip will be quite springy yet sturdy when rolled. Glue outer end in place as shown in finished pendant(page 91); this will be top where ring coil and jump ring will be located.

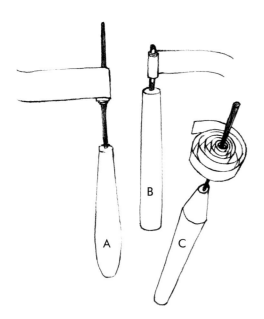

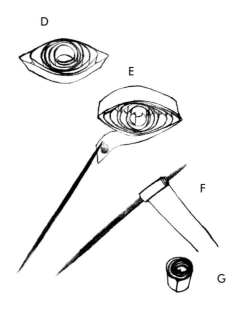

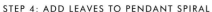

## STEP 4: ADD LEAVES TO PENDANT SPIRAL

Arrange and glue the thirty 3" (8cm) marquises on spiral, referring to finished pendant photograph as placement guide. Slightly stagger marquises on each side of spiral so they are not directly opposite one another, creating a slight sense of movement.

Make a cluster of 3 leaves using remaining 3 marquises by gluing the 2" (5cm) marquise between the two 2½" (6cm) marquises. Glue this cluster to end of spiral in center of pendant, as shown on pendant photograph.

## STEP 5: MAKE RING COIL

Roll a 3" (8cm) paper quilling strip that has torn ends (torn, rather than bluntly cut, will result in a smoother coil appearance) around tip of clean toothpick, resulting in coil with a center opening large enough to accommodate jump ring. Glue outer end in place.

Glue ring coil at spiral join spot.

## STEP 6: REINFORCE CONNECTIONS

Turn pendant over and apply small dots of glue on each spot where marquises are attached or coils joined. Allow glue to dry overnight before handling pendant.

## STEP 7: ADD JUMP RING AND NECKLACE CORD

Open jump ring by positioning ring with split at top and grasping each side of ring firmly with jewelry pliers. With a gentle twisting motion, pull one side forward while holding other side steady.

Thread open jump ring through ring coil at top of pendant.

Thread a necklace or cord of your choice through jump ring.

Close jump ring by grasping two sides with two pairs of jewelry pliers and bringing them back together to close circle.

## STEP 8: VARNISH PENDANT (OPTIONAL)

Depending on the project, Ann doesn't always find it necessary to protect her paper jewelry with any sort of coating as long as it is handled gently and not worn in the rain. If you prefer an extra layer of protection, however, you may add two coats of matte Liquitex Varnish, which will not take away from the natural look of paper.

To apply varnish, hold pendant by jump ring with one hand and brush on a thin, even coating using a small brush. Tape necklace cord across rim of a cup, suspending pendant in cup. Allow pendant to dry completely, and repeat process to add a second coat of varnish.

# DECORATIVE BOOKBINDINGS

For hundreds of years before the development of industrial book production methods, every book was individually bound and decorated by hand. After the pages were stitched within protective outer boards, these sturdy boards would be covered in leather, fabric, or paper decorated in a variety of ways.

Leather-bound books might boast patterns made by the application of a variety of small handmade brass finishing tools, each heated and applied by hand one at a time. If decorative elements were to appear in gold on a completed volume, the binder would press thin sheets of gold leaf onto the leather using the tool. A leather binding decorated in this way—with hundreds of individually applied leaves and branches—inspired paper filigree artist Ann Martin to create the curving, leafy pendant project on page 90.

One particularly lovely type of decorative book binding—especially breathtaking for those who embroider—is embroidered binding. Silk, satin, velvet, or even canvas was stitched with lustrous threads as well as luxurious metals and then used to cover a book's boards. Called "a peculiarly English art," these textile bindings were most popular in that country in the sixteenth and seventeenth centuries. Embroidered bindings seem fragile hundreds of years after they were made, but the skills of the embroiderer, the density of the stitching, and the use of sturdy metal embellishments have given these bindings a long life in libraries today.

Research libraries with special collections of rare books will often have examples of fine leather, textile, and other bindings reflecting the styles and tastes of the different places and eras in which they were created. As a result, a collection of decorative book bindings can offer a variety of design inspiration.

Although the age and fragile nature of historic book bindings in libraries means that they cannot often be handled, libraries are finding new ways to share these collections online. A curious designer can, for example, browse the bindings of the British Library without leaving home.

Below are suggestions for reading more about the history of bookbinding, browsing images of bindings and binding tools, and learning more about contemporary bookbinders and book artists:

*Encyclopedia of the Book*. Geoffrey Glaister. 2nd ed. New Castle, Delaware: Oak Knoll, 1996.

*The History of Decorated Bookbinding in England.* Howard M. Nixon and Mirjam Foot. New York: Oxford University Press, 1992.

*English Bookbinding Styles, 1450–1800: A Handbook*. David Pearson. Newcastle, Delaware: Oak Knoll, 2005.

*Embroidered Books*. Isobel Hall. London: Batsford; New York: Sterling, 2009.

*English Embroidered Bookbindings*. Cyril Davenport. New York: Dodd Mead and Co., 1899.

Inventory of Bookbinders' Finishing Tools at the Boston Athenaeum: www.bostonathenaeum.org/node/811

Folger Shakespeare Library's Bindings Database: http://luna.folger.edu/luna/servlet/BINDINGS~1~1

British Library's Bindings Database: www.bl.uk/catalogues/bookbindings/

Learn more about book bindings using these Subject Headings:

BOOKBINDING — HISTORY.
BINDINGS.
EMBROIDERED BINDINGS (BOOKBINDING).
LEATHER BINDINGS (BOOKBINDING).

# Arts and Crafts Ex Libris Set

## DESIGNED BY ANNA BONDOC

ABOUT THE ARTIST

Anna Bondoc lives and works in Los Angeles, where she is the founder and creative director of Anna Bondoc Design. She has written essays, taught English literature, and worked in a professional kitchen and a library as well. A teacher of art and design, Anna is the author of *Simply Paper Cutting: Hand-Cut Paper Projects for Home Decor, Stationery & Gifts.* You'll find her online at www.annabondoc.com.

Artist Anna Bondoc has long drawn inspiration from design movements of the past, including the Arts and Crafts movement. She decided to create a matching bookplate-bookmark set after browsing through several Arts and Crafts–era design books. The volumes she examined, all from the first decades of the twentieth century, extolled the virtues of handmade embellishment and featured designs taking inspiration from simple natural forms.

Anna's bookplate and matching bookmark are her modern take on the leafy, curvilinear forms popular in early twentieth-century design, and their layered structure provides a tactile, dimensional beauty. Her bookplate set allows you to add some creativity as you personalize a book you give as a gift. And the bookmark is made by "upcycling" the petal shapes cut from the parent bookplate, forming a one-of-a-kind way to mark your place.

These bookplates are a bit bulkier than traditional single-layer ones, but they work quite nicely in average-size hardcovers as well as in larger volumes (like many craft books). When adding any bookplate to a book, consider whether you might ever choose to remove it. If you anticipate removing the bookplate, use a special glue stick with removable adhesive to attach it.

BEYOND THIS PROJECT:

Anna's matched set enables you to add a handmade touch to any special book. If you're interested in making a large number of bookplates to outfit your entire library, you might consider creating a stamp or stencil to make production speedier (see page 87 for instructions on making a stamp, and page 121 to learn about making stencils). See page 100 for ways to learn more about the art and history of bookplates. And don't forget—family crests are a traditional element of bookplates, so you might also turn to page 169 for ideas on researching and designing your unique coat of arms.

## FINISHED DIMENSIONS

BOOKPLATE: 4 × 6" (10 × 15cm)

BOOKMARK: 2½ × 7" (6 × 18cm)

## SUPPLIES

- Cutting mat
- Metal ruler
- Pencil
- Craft knife with #11 craft knife blades
- 12" (30cm) square sheets of 80lb textured scrapbook cardstock in magenta, light teal, and pink
- 4 × 6" (10 × 15cm) piece transfer paper (optional)
- Craft glue
- Bone folder or spoon
- Adhesive pick-up square (an eraserlike cleaning square sold with paper arts and scrapbooking supplies)
- Fine-tip marker in color of choice
- Hole punch
- Tassel

## STEP 1: PREPARE CARDSTOCK

Using a cutting mat, metal ruler, pencil, and craft knife, measure and cut cardstock to following sizes:

- Three 4 × 6" (10 × 15cm) rectangles in magenta, light teal, and pink

- Two 2½ × 7" (6 × 18cm) rectangles in magenta and pink

## STEP 2: TRANSFER STENCIL

Photocopy bookplate Stencil A on page 99 at 160% and use scissors to cut around outside lines to form a 4 × 6" (10 × 15cm) rectangular stencil. On work surface, stack following layers in order, from bottom to top: light teal cardstock, transfer paper, stencil.

Hold the 3 layers in place with one hand, and trace over stencil shapes with pencil; transfer paper will imprint design onto cardstock. If you don't have transfer paper, shade entire back side of photocopied stencil with pencil, lay stencil on top of cardstock with shaded side down, and trace stencil design. Set aside transfer paper and stencil.

## STEP 3: CUT SHAPES FROM CARDSTOCK

On cutting mat, use craft knife to cut each shape from cardstock. Set aside petal shapes to use later for matching bookmark. To cut effectively, work from shoulder rather than wrist. Push down into cutting mat and pull knife through paper as you cut. Swivel wrist around corners and curves, using pinkie to pivot.

## STEP 4: ATTACH AND CUT SECOND LAYER

Lightly apply glue to back of first layer. Align it with magenta cardstock and glue the two together. Make sure layers are completely adhered with no gaps between them by burnishing surface: Gently rub cardstock surface in a back-and-forth motion using a bone folder or rounded back of spoon.

Using illustration B on page 99 as your guide, use a pencil to lightly draw the shapes on magenta cardstock (4 inner petals, 1 rectangle interior, and "x" and "i" interiors). On cutting mat, use craft knife to cut out each of these shapes.

## STEP 5: ATTACH THIRD (BACKING) LAYER

Lightly apply glue to back of second layer. Align it with pink cardstock and glue these layers together. Make sure layers are completely adhered with no gaps between them by burnishing surface as in Step 4.

Use adhesive pick-up square to remove any residual pencil and/or stray bits of glue. Allow bookplate to dry completely before using.

Using a fine-tip marker, write book owner's name inside bookplate's rectangular window.

## STEP 7: GATHER PREPARED PAPER FOR BOOKMARK

Gather light teal petals saved from Step 3, as well as the 2½ × 7" (6 × 18cm) magenta and pink rectangles you cut at start of project.

## STEP 8: GLUE PETALS IN PLACE

Use ruler and pencil to lightly draw an interior ⅛" (3mm) border within the 2½ × 7" (6 × 18cm) pink rectangle.

Using project photograph on page 97 as guide, arrange petal shapes within border, and glue in place.

## STEP 9: CREATE PINK BORDER

On pink layer, sketch a ⅛" (3mm) border around petal shapes, allowing border lines to connect with rectangle border you drew in Step 8. Cut out these shapes from pink layer with a craft knife, revealing design's negative space.

## STEP 10: ADD BACKING AND TASSEL

Lightly apply glue to back of pink layer. Align it with magenta 2½ × 7" (6 × 18cm) rectangle, and glue layers together. Make sure layers are completely adhered with no gaps between them by burnishing surface as in Step 4.

Use adhesive pick-up square to remove any residual pencil and/or stray bits of glue. Allow bookmark to dry completely, then use hole punch to create hole in top center edge, just inside pink frame. Thread tassel's top loop through hole, draw tassel through loop, and cinch gently to secure.

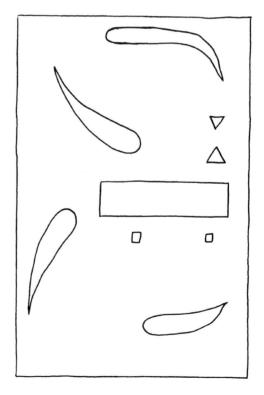

To make the bookplate and bookmark as shown on page 97, enlarge these both Stencil A (above left) and Illustration B (above right) by 160%.

# EX LIBRIS

A decorated square or rectangle of paper or cardstock pasted to a book's front endpaper, a bookplate's basic job is to identify who owns the book. But bookplates have long been more than simply functional; they often use graphics and symbols to offer a glimpse into the book owner's interests and background.

Bookplates first came into popular use in sixteenth-century Europe, when printed books began to be more accessible and libraries grew in number and size. Early bookplates incorporated coats of arms or family mottoes. Later, they began to reflect less formal elements of a book owner's personality, such as what they did for a living (a plant biologist might have a bookplate with a flower motif) or what kind of books they loved most (a silhouette of a child reading for a collector of children's books).

With a lovely ex libris (another word for bookplate, from the Latin for "from the books"), you can express your own interests and pursuits. If you're in search of bookplate inspiration, visit the following online library collections:

William Augustus Brewer Bookplate Collection, University of Delaware Library: http://fletcher.lib.udel.edu/collections/wab/index.htm

Ainslie Hewett Bookplate Collection, University of Louisville Libraries: http://digital.library.louisville.edu/cdm/landingpage/collection/hewett

John Starr Stewart Ex Libris Collection, University of Illinois at Urbana-Champaign Library: http://images.library.illinois.edu/projects/exlibris

Leah Mishkin Bookplate Collection, Jewish Theological Seminary Library: www.jtsa.edu/The_Library/Collections/Bookplate_Collection.xml

Pratt Institute Libraries Bookplate Collection: www.flickr.com/photos/prattinstitutelibraries/sets/72157613160345964

Included among the books artist Anna Bondoc used in her search for bookplate inspiration are:

*The Bookplates and Badges of C. F. A. Voysey: Architect and Designer of the Arts and Crafts Movement.* Karen Livingstone. Woodbridge, Suffolk: Antique Collectors' Club, 2011.

*Practical Stencil Work: A Guide to Designing and Cutting Stencils and Executing Stencil Work for All Purposes.* Frederick Scott-Mitchell. London: Trade Papers Pub. Co., 1906.

*Designing from Plant Forms.* John W. Wadsworth. London: Chapman., 1910.

To find similar books on bookplates, use these Subject Headings:

ART IN BOOKPLATES.

BOOKPLATES.

DECORATION AND ORNAMENT — PLANT STENCIL WORK.

FORMS.

GEOGRAPHY IN BOOKPLATES.

HERALDIC BOOKPLATES.

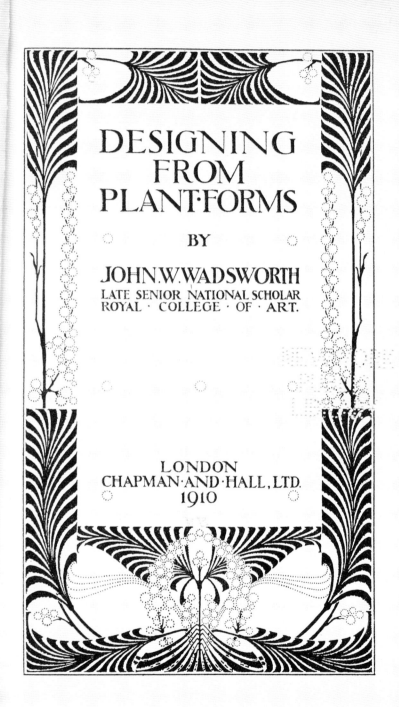

# DESIGNING FROM PLANT·FORMS

BY

## JOHN. W. WADSWORTH

LATE SENIOR NATIONAL SCHOLAR
ROYAL · COLLEGE · OF · ART.

LONDON
CHAPMAN·AND·HALL, LTD.
1910

ABOVE In *Designing from Plant Forms*, plants are presented first as they appear in nature and then transformed into art nouveau designs.

# Cross-Stitch Wall Panel

## DESIGNED BY HALEY PIERSON-COX

ABOUT THE ARTIST
Haley Pierson-Cox is
a staff writer at *CRAFT
Magazine* and a review
contributor for *Craft Test
Dummies* and she also
cohosts Craft Social, a
monthly craft-centered
Twitter chat. She is a
self-described technical
craft writing and tutorial-
obsessed book nerd who
designs DIY projects
and blogs about crafts,
handmade geekery, and
all things domestic at
www.thezenofmaking.com.

Richly embellished lettering of all kinds was what first drew crafter Haley Pierson-Cox to her library. From illuminated manuscripts to century-old sign painters' manuals, each source offered her a glimpse of the roots of the art of hand lettering. To honor the variety and beauty of illuminated and hand-embellished lettering, Haley designed a large-format cross-stitch wall panel that draws inspiration from historical illuminated letters while bringing them into a modern living space.

Her panel's design was the result of studying a wide variety of materials, including online sources like the British Library's Illuminated Manuscripts site. And while Haley chose her color palette from the jewel-like tones of early illuminated manuscripts, it was a "modern treatise" from 1911, *The Standard American Drawing and Lettering Book* by Peter Idarius, that provided the inspiration for her blossoming cross-stitch letterforms.

Cross-stitch is one of the easiest embroidery stitches to learn. In this project, Haley combines basic cross-stitches with horizontal and vertical border stitches on pegboard.

BEYOND THIS PROJECT:

Haley designed illuminated letters for just one word, READ. But you could use her forms as a starting point to create cross-stitch patterns for the rest of the alphabet, and then stitch a sign with whatever word or name you wish.

You could also use her cross-stitch pattern as the basis for a traditional cross-stitch work on cloth. Or, you might create a bookmark by stitching the pattern onto perforated cross-stitch paper with just a strand or two of embroidery thread to keep the bookmark from getting too bulky.

If you'd like to pursue illuminated manuscript inspiration, see page 109 for ideas about where to view images online and how to find books about them at the library.

- 24 × 48" (61 × 122cm)

## SUPPLIES

- One 24 × 48" (61 × 122cm) pegboard sheet with a 1" (2.5cm) square grid
- Paper towels
- Rubbing alcohol
- Newspaper or dropcloth
- 1 quart (1 liter) paint in light matte gray
- Paint stirrer
- Paint tray
- Paint roller, high density for smooth surfaces
- Scissors
- 125 yards (115 meters) super bulky yarn in navy
- 50 yards (46 meters) each of super bulky yarn in green, red, and gold
- Extra-large darning needle
- Toothpick (optional)
- Masking tape
- Four 1½" (4cm)-wide by ¾" (2cm)-thick by 3" (8cm)-long wooden blocks (soft pine is recommended, to avoid drilling)
- One 1½" (4cm)-wide by ¾" (2cm)-thick by 12" (30cm)-long wooden block (soft pine is recommended, to avoid drilling)
- Fourteen ½" (12mm) wood screws
- Screwdriver
- 2 wire strap hangers
- Braided hanging wire (at least 30lb [14kg] test), at least 50" (127cm) in length
- 2 screws for hanging on wall (check with the experts at your local hardware store if you're not sure what will work with your walls)
- Pencil
- Ruler or tape measure
- Level
- Drill (for installing screws in wall)

### STEP 1: PREPARE PEGBOARD SURFACE FOR PAINTING

Gently wipe down front (coated side) of pegboard with a paper towel dampened with rubbing alcohol to remove any grease or dust from surface. Allow to dry.

Spread newspaper or a dropcloth on floor, then place pegboard in center with front side facing up.

### STEP 2: PAINT PEGBOARD

Stir paint thoroughly to make sure it is well mixed. Pour a small amount of paint into paint tray. Evenly saturate roller with paint, removing any excess liquid by rolling paint roller down slant of tray a few times before using.

Apply first layer of paint to pegboard using even up-and-down strokes.

Continue adding layers of paint, allowing each coat to dry completely before adding a new one, until color is smooth and completely opaque. Add more paint to tray as needed.

Allow painted pegboard to dry for at least 24 hours before proceeding.

### STEP 3: STITCH BLUE CROSS-STITCHES

Note: When cross-stitching on pegboard, keep in mind that each square on the pattern corresponds with 4 holes on the pegboard that together make up the corners of a 1" (2.5cm) square.

A single cross-stitch is made by inserting the needle into the back of the fabric (or pegboard) at the bottom left corner, then stitching diagonally across the front of the square and into the top right corner. This diagonal stitch is then crossed by inserting the needle into the back of the "fabric" at bottom right corner and then stitching diagonally across the front to the top left corner.

The stitches in this project are worked in the following order: First, all diagonal stitches and cross-stitches are worked. Only after these are completed do you stitch the vertical and horizontal outline stitches around the letters, flowers, and leaves.

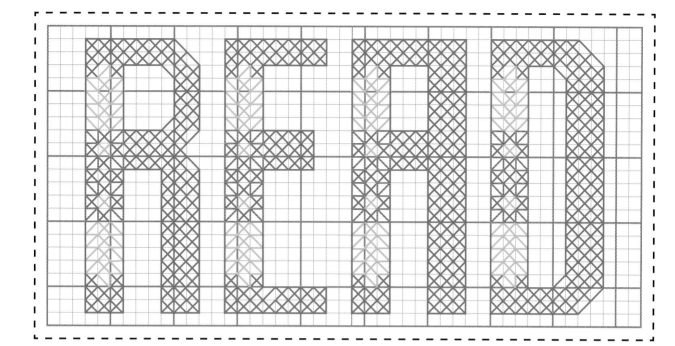

To make stitching easier, prop up pegboard between two chairs to give you equal access to both front and back of work. Also, it helps to stick the blunt end of a toothpick through the hole before each stitch to help you find the right stitching location on the back.

Cut a 2 to 3-yard length of blue yarn and thread one end through eye of darning needle.

Using chart above as well as photograph of finished project as a guide, locate square on pegboard where upper left corner of R will be placed. (Note that there is a border of unstitched squares that surrounds lettering.)

Insert needle from back to front of pegboard through hole at bottom left corner of that square. Pull yarn through to front of board, leaving a 2 to 3" tail of yarn at back. Use a small piece of masking tape to fasten yarn end to back of board, taking care to avoid covering any holes.

Next, insert needle from front to back of pegboard through hole that is in upper right corner of that square, pulling yarn through.

You should now have a single diagonal line through the square.

Cross-stitches are generally worked in horizontal rows instead of being completed individually, so you will do a series of matching bottom-left-to-top-right diagonal stitches in each square that should contain a cross-stitch.

Following grid on chart, continue on from left to right in a straight horizontal row, stitching each square marked with a blue X on chart with a bottom-left-to-top-right diagonal stitch.

Be sure to skip squares that are blank on chart, as well as squares at corners of the R and D that are marked on chart to be stitched with just a single diagonal going in opposite direction.

When skipping squares that are blank on chart, simply allow the yarn to lie flat horizontally across back of pegboard and continue on to next square.

When you reach end of first row, insert needle into bottom right hole in the square just to right of the one you've just stitched, pulling yarn from back to front. Finish this stitch by

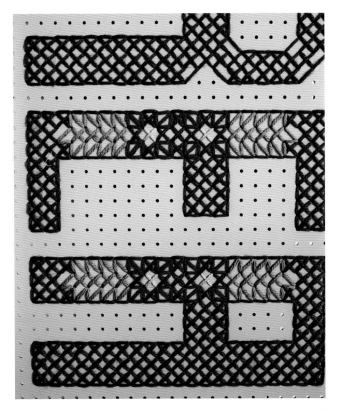

inserting needle into upper left hole of square, pulling yarn from front to back.(On the chart, this square gets a single bottom-right-to-top-left diagonal stitch.)

Insert needle from back to front through hole directly below the one you just stitched, pulling yarn to front and finishing this stitch by inserting needle into upper left hole of square, pulling yarn from front to back.

Continue along row from right to left, crossing the rest of the stitches in same way with bottom-right-to-top-left diagonal stitches.

Be sure to stitch square at corner of the R with a single bottom-right-to-top-left diagonal stitch, just as you did with the corner of the D.

Using method above and continuing to follow chart, continue stitching horizontal rows of blue cross-stitches in same manner until you reach end of chart.

When you run out of yarn, don't knot it off. Use your needle to run yarn end behind a few stitches on back to secure it in place without adding bulk. Use same trick to secure end of new piece of yarn before you continue stitching.

## STEP 4: STITCH GREEN, RED, AND GOLD CROSS-STITCHES

Follow same process used for blue yarn to stitch cross-stitches with green, red, and gold yarn, following chart.

Just as with the corners R and D in blue above, some of the green and red stitches in chart contain only one diagonal stitch, not a complete cross-stitch. Just keep an eye on chart and work whatever diagonals are called for, and don't cross them.

## STEP 5: STITCH HORIZONTAL AND VERTICAL STITCHES

Following chart as a guide, use a straight stitch to complete individual horizontal and vertical stitches along edges of leaves and flower petals.

Following chart, use a backstitch to create an outline around each letter as follows: Starting at bottom left corner of letter R and working vertically up side, bring needle from back to front through lowest hole (Hole A). Make a straight stitch on front into next hole above it (Hole B). Bring needle back up from back to front through next hole above Hole B (Hole C), and then back down through Hole B. Bring needle back up from back to front through next hole above Hole C (Hole D), and then back down through Hole C. This will create an unbroken line of stitches.

Continue backstitching entire length of outline.

## STEP 6: INSTALL HANGING WIRE

Note: This is a heavy piece. If you're unsure about how best to secure it to your wall, head over to your local hardware store and ask an expert—it's always best to play it safe!

Position pegboard flat on floor with front side facing up.

Place one small wooden block under each of the four corners of pegboard, aligning long edges of each wooden rectangle with top or bottom edge of pegboard. (The wooden blocks will be on back side of finished piece.)

Using holes in the pegboard as your guide, secure wooden blocks in place through front of pegboard using two screws in each block.

Next, center 12"-long wooden block between the two blocks along top edge, then screw it in place through front using 4 evenly spaced screws. This large piece will stabilize pegboard, preventing it from bowing in center when finished project is hung on the wall.

(If desired, you can use extra paint to cover tops of screws when you're finished.)

Once blocks are secured, carefully turn pegboard over and place it face down on a clean dropcloth or blanket to protect its front surface. Use two remaining wood screws to attach wire strap hangers to center of two small corner blocks at top corners of pegboard.

Attach hanging wire to wire strap hangers per instructions on hanging wire package, allowing wire to pass beneath center bracing block. Pull wire taut across back.

With wire under center block, you will have a place on each side to hang pegboard.

## STEP 7: HANG PEGBOARD

To hang pegboard, you will need to install two screws into your wall (talk to an expert at your local hardware store if you're not sure which screws to use).

Use a pencil to mark place on wall where you'd like top-center of piece to fall. Then, using a ruler and level, make marks 14" to left and 14" to right of center mark. Measure distance from floor to each of these points, making sure that left, right, and center marks all measure same distance, then install two screws in wall at two marks you made 14" from center. You may need a drill for this step, depending on composition of your walls.

Once screws are securely in place, hang cross-stitch wall art across both screws using hanging wire on back of piece.

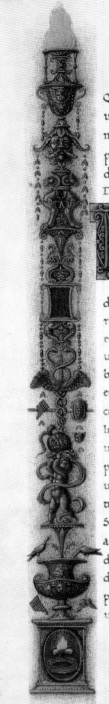

Quorum eximio fulgore multum cerimoniis nostris
inclite claritatis accessit. Deos enim reliquos accepi
mus. Caesares dedimus: et quia initium a cultu deor̄
petere in animo est: de condictione eius summatim
dis      s      e      r      a      m:

DE CVLTV DEORVM CAPITVLVM I·

AIORES STATAS SOLENESQ
cerimonias pontificum scientia benege
rendarum rerum auctoritate auguriũ
obseruatione apollinis praedicatione ua
tum libris portentorum depulsis etrusc
disciplina explicari uoluerunt. Prisco etiam instituto
rebus diuinis opera datur cum aliquid comendandũ
est precatione: cum exposcendum uoto: cum soluend
um gratulatione: cum inquirendum extis uel sorti
bus impartito solenni ritu peragendum sacrificio qũ
etiam ostentorum ac fulgurum denunciationes pro
curantur. Tantum autem studium antiquis non so
lum seruandae sed etiam amplificandae religionis fui
ut florentissima tum & opulentissima cuitate decem
principum filijs Senatus consulto singulis etruriae pop
ulis percipiendae sacrorum disciplinae gratia traderē
tur: Cererique quam more greco uenerari instituerāt
Sacerdotem Auelia: cum id opidum non dum cuitatis
accepisset nomen Calcitrariam peterent. Vel ut alij
dicunt Caliphenam: Ne deae uetustis ritibus perita
deess& antistes cuius cum in urbe pulcerrimum tem
plum haberetur greco ritu moniti sibillinis libris ut
uetustissimam Cererem placarent Hennam quoniã

# ILLUMINATED MANUSCRIPTS

Any individual illuminated manuscript from the Middle Ages or the Renaissance is many things at one time—a handwritten book, a work of art, a priceless antiquarian object, an example of material culture and craftsmanship, an entire herd of goats, and a rare and special text.

Often created by monks in a scriptorium, these volumes were made of sheets of vellum (scraped and prepared animal skins) on which text was written using a quill pen. These pages were embellished with designs in burnished gold leaf and colorful inks made from ground minerals or plant dyes. Every illuminated manuscript was unique.

Libraries that hold these volumes take their stewardship quite seriously, and many have retired these treasures from active use in order to protect their vulnerable colors from overexposure. But luckily for us, many libraries have also ensured that their illuminated manuscripts can be viewed online, so that the curious browser has quite a bit of inspiration at her fingertips. You may not be able to read the texts: Even if the manuscript is written in a language you know, the letterforms might be difficult to recognize. But don't let that stop you from peeking into the world of illuminated manuscripts. You may want to examine the illuminated letterforms, or explore the illustrated frames as well as the full scenes that some volumes contain.

From whimsical animal forms to religious figures, illuminated manuscripts reward careful examination. And what you discover might lead to a new sketch, an embroidery design, a collage element, or something entirely unexpected. Here are just a few of the online library sites devoted to illuminated manuscripts:

Penn in Hand: Selected Medieval and Renaissance Manuscripts at the University of Pennsylvania's Rare Book and Manuscript Library: http://dla.library.upenn.edu/dla/medren/index.html

Virtual Manuscript Library of Switzerland: www.e-codices.unifr.ch/de

British Library's Illuminated Manuscripts: www.bl.uk/catalogues/illuminatedmanuscripts/tours.asp

Digital Scriptorium, A Collaborative Tool for Studying Medieval and Renaissance Manuscripts: from Many Institutions: http://scriptorium.columbia.edu/

UCLA Directory of Digitized Manuscripts Online: http://manuscripts.cmrs.ucla.edu/index.php

And if you'd like to identify books about illuminated manuscripts and hand-drawn letter arts, here are some Subject Headings to get you started:

> ALPHABETS.
> BOOK ORNAMENTATION.
> ILLUMINATION OF BOOKS AND
>     MANUSCRIPTS.
> LETTERING.
> SIGN PAINTING.

If you are particularly interested in early manuscript letterforms, you might also want to learn more about the history of type design (page 88) and about penmanship resources (page 80).

# Kitten Pockets Dress— and Kittens!

## DESIGNED BY HEATHER ROSS AND JESSICA PIGZA

ABOUT THE ARTIST
Heather Ross is an illustrator, author, and textile designer. She is the author of *Weekend Sewing* and *Heather Ross Prints*, and she illustrates the Crafty Chloe picture book series as well. She lives and works in New York City, and you'll find her online at heatherross .squarespace.com.

Lots of the work that happens in libraries is collaborative. Readers consult with librarians and curators about how best to find answers to their questions. Librarians from one institution collaborate with those at another to create new discovery tools or to virtually reunite collections that are divided among libraries. Librarians work with teachers to create classes, and students work on projects as a team. In the case of this project, an unexpected but incredibly fun collaboration resulted from an illustrator's inspired dress design paired with a librarian's idea to create matching embroidered kitten companions.

The library book that sparked designer and illustrator Heather Ross's idea was a 1922 edition of *Heidi*, the classic novel by Johanna Spyri about a young waif who shows her grumpy Alpine-dwelling grandfather that there's more to love in life than just goats. What made this edition so memorable to Heather were the illustrations by Jessie Willcox Smith. Smith knew her way around children and animals and earned a reputation for her full-hearted depictions of these creatures. After studying one illustration in particular—of Heidi carrying kittens in her pockets—Heather knew she wanted to create a sweet dress with two pockets for carrying precious items like Heidi did. My own kittens seemed a natural addition to the project, and I based their embroidered expression on one of Heather's own illustrations, of a sleepy, contented cat at sea with her owl companion.

The illustrations in the1922 edition of *Heidi* highlight the young heroine's love for all creatures.

BEYOND THIS PROJECT:

If you know a little one who likes kittens, make an entire litter for her, and by enlarging the template you can make a mother cat as well. You could also use leftover fabric scraps from sewing your child's clothes to make a variety of tiny soft toys to match his or her handmade wardrobe. If you'd like to browse more illustrations from this edition of *Heidi* to see how inspiration strikes you, you can view them on the New York Public Library's website. And if you're interested in exploring other children's books with an eye to potential new craft inspiration, check out the ideas on page 116.

- Dress: 19" (48cm) long (not including straps), 22" (56cm) around the top
- Kittens: 6 × 2½" (15 × 6cm)

## SUPPLIES

- 1 yard (91cm) cotton fabric for dress and kittens
- ¼ yard (23cm) each of two to three coordinating cotton fabrics for dress straps and kittens
- ¼ yard (23cm) iron-on adhesive, such as Heat'n Bond Lite
- 2 yards (183cm) ⅜" (1cm)–wide elastic or velvet elastic
- Measuring tape
- Tailor's chalk
- Fabric scissors
- Iron
- Ironing board
- Sewing machine
- Threads to match fabrics and elastic
- Pins
- Small pointed object like knitting needle
- Fiberfill
- Dressmaker's tracing paper
- Embroidery floss
- Hand sewing-needle
- Craft scissors

Note: The dress can be customized to fit lots of little girls by adjusting the length and circumference of the main body of the dress.

## STEP 1: PREPARE AND CUT FABRICS FOR DRESS

Wash, dry, and press all fabrics.

Cut main body of dress: Fold main dress fabric in half, with wrong side facing out and selvage edges together. Measure and mark a rectangle 23" (58cm) along fold and 19" (48cm) across. Cut out this rectangle.

Cut dress straps: From fabric of your choice, cut 2 fabric strips, each 11" (28cm) long and 2½" (6cm) wide.

Cut pockets: From main dress fabric, cut 2 rectangles, each 10½ × 5½" (27 × 14cm).

## STEP 2: SEW BODY OF DRESS

Fold main dress fabric rectangle in half, wrong side facing out, lining up the 23" (58cm) edges together. Using a sewing machine and leaving a ½" (1.2cm) seam allowance, sew along the 23" (58cm)-long side to form a tube of fabric. Press seam. Finish raw edges of fabric with a serger, if desired. This seam will be at center back of finished dress.

All around top of tube, fold a 1" (2.5cm)-wide edge of fabric to inside and press. Turn this same edge down another inch (2.5cm), hiding raw edge, and press again. Use a sewing machine to sew a basting line ¾" (2cm) from top edge, securing folded fabric down.

The next task is to add elastic to form dress's gathered top. If you're unfamiliar with stitching elastic, you might want to practice on scrap fabric with extra elastic first.

Cut a 24" (61cm)-long piece of elastic. Position one end of elastic right at back center seam and line it up so that it covers basting seam.

Switch sewing machine to zigzag stitch and thread machine with a color that matches your elastic. Using a walking foot is helpful if you have one, but not necessary. Place elastic end positioned over back center seam under foot of sewing machine and carefully lower foot. Working slowly and carefully, backstitch once or twice to secure elastic to dress.

Then, gently pull elastic both in front and behind, stretching it along the dress fabric covering over the basting seam, and sew a line of zigzag stitches along length of elastic all the way around dress until you meet starting point at center back. Take your time.

When you reach starting point, overlap the elastic at center back by about ½" (1.2cm), stitch through both elastic layers, and backstitch a few times to secure it. You may find that your elastic is a bit longer than needed to reach overlap point. If so, simply complete overlapping backstitches and carefully trim off any extra elastic not sewn down.

## STEP 3: MAKE POCKETS

Fold one pocket rectangle in half, with wrong side facing out and short edges together. Using a sewing machine and leaving a ½" (1.2cm) seam allowance, sew around the three open sides, but leave a 2" (5cm) turning opening along side opposite folded edge.

Turn pocket right side out through turning opening and press it flat, turning edge of turning opening under ½" (1.2cm). Hand-stitch turning opening closed using blind stitch.

Cut an 8" (20cm) length of elastic. Position it 1" (2.5cm) below folded edge of pocket, running parallel to that folded edge, and centered so that extra elastic hangs off both sides. Pin elastic in center.

Confirm that sewing machine is still set to zigzag stitch and thread in machine matches elastic. Using a walking foot is helpful if you have one, but not necessary. Position pocket and elastic under foot of sewing machine and carefully lower foot. Working slowly, backstitch once or twice to secure elastic on pocket edge. Then, gently pull elastic both in front and behind, stretching it along pocket fabric, and sew a line of zigzag stitches along length of elastic all the way to opposite edge of pocket. Take your time and

remove pin as you approach it. When you reach opposite end of pocket, backstitch elastic to edge of pocket fabric.

Trim elastic ends so they extend just ½" (1.2cm) beyond pocket on both sides.

Turn elastic ends around to wrong side of pocket edge and stitch them down with a few small hand-stitches.

Repeat process with second pocket rectangle to make second pocket.

## STEP 4: ADD POCKETS TO DRESS

Spread dress out flat on work surface, right side out and with front (side without long center seam) facing up.

Position pockets just along right and left front edges of dress, with their bottoms approximately 9" (23cm) above lower dress edge. (It's natural that pockets will be wider at bottom than the top, because of gathering effect of elastic.) Pin pockets in place.

Use blind stitch to hand-stitch pockets in place around sides and bottom, allowing ruffled top portion (the portion of pocket above elastic band) to remain free.

## STEP 5: HEM DRESS

Fold a 1" (2.5cm)-wide hem to inside of dress and press. Turn this same edge in again, hiding raw edge, and press again. Machine-sew a seam $^3/_4$" (2cm) from hem edge, securing hem. Or, if you prefer, hand-stitch hem using a hem stitch.

## STEP 6: ADD STRAPS TO DRESS

Fold each 11 × 2½" (28 × 6cm) fabric strip in half lengthwise, right sides together.

Use a sewing machine to sew fabric closed along long edge of each folded strip, with a ¼" (5mm) seam allowance. Turn each strap right side out; you may wish to use a knitting needle to gently turn the strap.

Press each strap flat, positioning seam running down center of one side.

Making sure that seams of straps face down, pin straps so that fronts are attached to inside of dress approximately 3 to 4" (8 to 10cm) to left and right of center front, and backs are attached 3 to 4" (8 to 10cm) to left and right of center back. (You may wish to try it on your little girl at this point to adjust straps for a custom fit.) Hand-stitch straps in place, securing strap ends with stitches along wrong side of row of zigzag stitches so stitches won't be visible on right side of dress.

### STEP 7: CUT OUT KITTEN PIECES

Make two photocopies of template on page 115 at 105%. Using scissors, cut kitten body from one and kitten belly and ears from the other.

Use kitten body template as guide to cut 2 kitten bodies from fabric of your choice.

Trace kitten belly and ears templates onto paper cover of a piece of iron-on adhesive. Follow manufacturer's instructions and iron adhesive to wrong side of piece of fabric you want to use to make belly and ears. After the adhesive cools, cut out all 3 pieces along template lines drawn on paper.

### STEP 8: ATTACH KITTEN BELLY AND EARS

Carefully peel off paper layer of adhesive from belly and ears. Using kitten body template as a guide to placement, position belly and ears, adhesive side down, on a kitten body. Follow manufacturer's instructions and iron adhesive to secure belly and ears to kitten body.

Using your sewing machine and thread to match belly and ear fabric, carefully sew around edges of belly and ears, $1/8$" from raw edge.

### STEP 9: EMBROIDER KITTEN FACE

Place kitten body, face up, on work surface. Place a small piece of dressmaker's tracing paper over it, and place kitten body template on top, positioning it so face is where you want it to be on fabric kitten body.

Use a small pointed object like a knitting needle to trace over eyes, nose, and mouth. This will transfer face design onto fabric kitten body.

Using 2 strands of embroidery floss, stitch eyes and mouth using backstitch and the nose with satin stitch.

### STEP 10: COMPLETE KITTEN

Place the 2 kitten bodies right sides together. Using your sewing machine and thread to match the kitten body, carefully sew all around edge of kitten body, leaving a ¼" (5mm) seam allowance and leaving bottom open.

Turn kitten right side out, using a small object like a knitting needle to gently turn out ears. Stuff kitten with fiberfill, being sure to work stuffing all the way up into ears. Whipstitch opening closed.

Repeat steps 7 to 10 to make as many kittens as you wish.

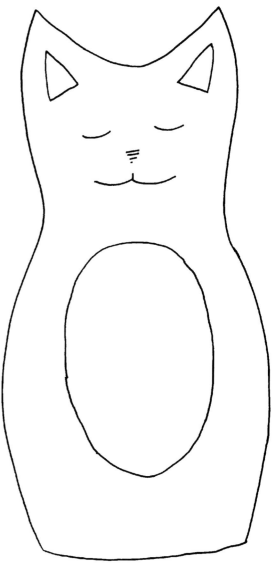

# CHILDREN'S BOOKS

Do you find yourself idly hunting for favorite books from your youth when wandering in used book stores? Do you have a weakness for historical children's book illustration? You aren't alone. Regardless of whether your tastes run to *The Phantom Tollbooth*, *Frog and Toad*, *A Wrinkle in Time*, or *Harriet the Spy*, there are special collections in libraries and staff experts devoted to the history of children's books. Interested readers and researchers can search libraries to see if a beloved old edition of a favorite tale is out there waiting to offer fresh inspiration.

Often, libraries with historical children's book collections will seek out multiple editions of the same work. The University of Florida's Baldwin Library, for instance, is known for its comparative copies of texts like *Robinson Crusoe* and *Alice in Wonderland*. These gatherings of multiple editions allow a library to document the changing ways a story has been presented and experienced by readers; and for users, it provides an opportunity to search for the specific copy, with the exact illustrations, they remember from childhood. It was through her rediscovery of a favorite old copy of the classic tale of *Heidi*—one published in 1922, with illustrations by Jessie Willcox Smith—that artist and illustrator Heather Ross found design inspiration for her project (see page 110).

Beyond just texts, libraries with children's literature collections may also have in their collections movable books, pop-up books, games, toys, puzzles, and perhaps even original artwork and manuscripts. For example, the Cotsen Library at Princeton University has digitized pages from Père Castor's hands-on activity books, including details on how young readers could make a menagerie of articulated paper animals. If you're interested in tracking down vintage copies of memorable children's books, discovering new favorite books and activities, or reading more about the history of children's books, try the following libraries online to get started:

Children's Literature at the Library of Congress: www.loc.gov/rr/rarebook/digitalcoll/digitalcoll-children.html

Cotsen Children's Library at Princeton University: www.princeton.edu/cotsen

Baldwin Library of Historic Children's Literature, at the University of Florida: http://ufdc.ufl.edu/?c=juv

University of Pittsburgh's 19th Century Schoolbooks: http://digital.library.pitt.edu/nietz

Harvard Views of Readers, Readership, and Reading History: http://ocp.hul.harvard.edu/reading/textbooks.html

These guides can help you discover more about children's books:

*Minders of Make-Believe: Idealists, Entrepreneurs, and the Shaping of American Children's Literature.* Leonard S. Marcus. Boston: Houghton Mifflin Co., 2008.

*Children's Book Illustration and Design.* Julie Cummins, ed. New York: Library of Applied Design, PC International, 1992.

And these Library of Congress Subject Headings will lead to even more references:

ILLUSTRATED CHILDREN'S BOOKS.

ILLUSTRATION OF BOOKS.

ILLUSTRATORS — BIOGRAPHY.

PICTURE BOOKS FOR CHILDREN.

TOY AND MOVABLE BOOKS.

In Willebeek Le Mair's *Children's Corner* (1915), even the littlest girls are creative and industrious.

# Cyanotype Throw

## DESIGNED BY NATALIE CHANIN

ABOUT THE ARTIST
Natalie Chanin is the founder and creative director of Alabama Chanin and the author of *Alabama Stitch Book*, *Alabama Studio Style*, and *Alabama Studio Sewing + Design*. Her work has been featured in *Vogue*, the *New York Times*, and *Town & Country*, among many other publications, as well as on CBS News. She is a member of the Council of Fashion Designers of America. She lives and works in her hometown of Florence, Alabama. You'll find her online at www .alabamachanin.com.

When designer Natalie Chanin started thinking about research topics to explore in library collections, botany, Alabama natural history, and poetry were all on her reading list. And each of these elements informed her finished design for a stenciled, embroidered throw completed in her signature style using organic cotton jersey.

Natalie's stencil, with its hovering moth, arose from her study of illustrations from the pages of *Letters from Alabama*, written by English traveler Philip Henry Gosse. Gosse left his home in Worcester, England, in 1838 to spend eight months in Pleasant Hill, Alabama, and that book was one of numerous works in which he explored his lifelong love of insects, plants, and flowers. And it was Anna Atkins's landmark nineteenth-century photographic work, *Photographs of British Algae*, that gave rise to Natalie's color choices. Atkins, a botanist in England who learned about the cyanotype photography process from its inventor, Sir John Herschel, used the process to create vivid images of sea plants. To these design elements Natalie added words, in the form of a poem by Cecily Parks called "Luna Moth."

BEYOND THIS PROJECT:

Because the stencil is used as a repeating pattern, it is small enough on its own to be applied to smaller-in-scale projects like a pillow, scarf, skirt, or home goods. To learn more about the design directions you can take using Natalie's stencils on clothing, home goods, accessories, and paper arts, and to see more options on embellishment (using beads, embroidery, and other hand-sewing techniques), see Natalie's books: *Alabama Stitch Book*, *Alabama Studio Style*, and *Alabama Studio Sewing + Design*.

If you'd like to study botanical illustration with an eye to creating your own stencil, see page 124 for suggested sources and research volumes. You could create a stencil design incorporating your favorite leaves or flower shapes, or using plants native to a place that's meaningful to you.

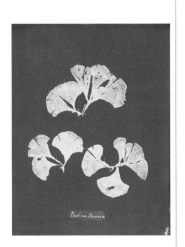

LEFT Nineteenth-century cyanotypes of sea plants informed Natalie's design.

FINISHED DIMENSIONS
- 85 × 60" (216 × 152cm)

SUPPLIES
- Spray adhesive
- 18 × 24" (46 × 61cm) sheet clear acetate, posterboard, or acrylic pennant felt, for stencil
- Craft knife
- Cutting mat
- One 85 × 60" (216 × 152cm) piece medium-weight organic cotton jersey fabric in blue
- Tailor's chalk
- Yardstick
- Dropcloth
- Painter's tape (optional)
- Butcher paper, for masking fabric while stenciling (optional)
- Textile paint in gold
- Stencil brush, sponge, or clean spray bottle with adjustable nozzles, to apply textile paint to fabric
- Black ultrafine permanent marker
- Scraps of organic cotton jersey fabric in yellow and black
- 4" (10cm) embroidery scissors
- 5" (13cm) knife-edge sewing and craft scissors
- Sewing needle
- Straight pins
- Coats & Clark Dual Duty Button & Craft Thread in black and dogwood
- Embroidery floss in black and gold

STEP 1: MAKE STENCIL
Photocopy and enlarge the stencil template on page 123 by 400% so it measures 15½" (39cm) across at its widest point.

Use spray adhesive to affix enlarged stencil design to stenciling material of your choice.

Place stenciling material with its attached design, face up, on a cutting mat. Use craft knife to cut out all black areas of stencil design. Work carefully and slowly to avoid injury.

You may wish to test stencil before transferring image to your project fabric. To do so, lay stencil on top of a piece of paper or acetate, and transfer stencil design following instructions below. The resulting image shows exactly how stencil will look on fabric. You've also created a backup image that can be cut into a new stencil if original gets lost or damaged.

STEP 2: MAP OUT DESIGN
Spread throw fabric out fully on floor or a large work surface. Use tailor's chalk and a yardstick to map out placement of stencils on throw.

Measure and mark a 16" (41cm) margin across top of throw fabric and 4" (10cm) margins on sides and bottom edge.

Next, mark out a grid within confines of margins. Grid should consist of 9 rectangles, each measuring 17" (43cm) wide by 21½" (55cm) tall.

Edges of throw will be left raw because they will eventually roll nicely and create their own border.

STEP 3: STENCIL FABRIC
Cover floor or work surface with dropcloth and spread out prepared throw base on it. Smooth out any wrinkles.

Position stencil in center of top left rectangle of grid.

Use painter's tape, if desired, to secure stencil to fabric and prevent it from shifting. You may also wish to use butcher's paper to mask off fabric around your active stenciling area to protect it from stray paint.

Using gold fabric paint and stencil brush, sponge, or spray bottle, carefully transfer stencil design to fabric by dabbing paint in each of stencil's cut-out shapes or spraying paint through stencil opening. When you've finished painting entire stencil, remove it from fabric, being careful not to transfer any paint left on stencil, and let paint dry to the touch.

Repeat stenciling within 8 remaining rectangles of the grid.

### STEP 4: ADD POETRY EXCERPT

Once stenciling is completely dry, use a permanent marker to add words, if you wish. Natalie chose an excerpt from "Luna Moth" by Cecily Parks (see full poem at right) and added the writing in freehand. Here are the lines she used, along with notes about their location on the project:

[above row one]
    Pale green and pressed against the
        window screen,
    shot through with field, you watch
        nighttime's corners
    curl with four white eyes, your under-
    self unfurled...

[between rows one and two]
    knife block. Having lived one of your
        life's
    six nights, you leave a limp
        silhouette where you

[between rows two and three]
    left off—let me be the creature
        circling
    your sleep. I am the most benign
        unknown.

[below row three]
    —Cecily Parks

If you are not comfortable using your own handwriting on your throw, see page 152 for ideas on how to use a word processing program to create lettering instead.

### STEP 5: CUT OUT APPLIQUÉ SHAPES FROM CONTRASTING FABRICS

Using stencil and tailor's chalk, trace stencil shapes you would like to use for appliqué from the scrap fabrics. Cut out the shapes with scissors and pin them to your base fabric. Pin each shape over its corresponding shape on painted stencils on throw. Cut out and pin as many or as few shapes as you want.

### STEP 6: APPLIQUÉ SHAPES IN PLACE

Use Button & Craft thread to attach each appliqué shape to base fabric using parallel whipstitch along edge of shape, making the stitches and spaces between them both $3/8$" (1cm).

### STEP 7: CHAIN-STITCH WORDS AND STEMS

Use 4 strands of embroidery floss to go over the words with chain stitches.

If desired, go over some of the stem lines with 4 strands of embroidery floss and chain stitches as well.

LUNA MOTH

Pale green and pressed against the window screen,
shot through with field, you watch nighttime's corners
curl with four white eyes, your underself unfurled
to my one room of world—kettle, counter,

knife block. Having lived one of your life's
six nights, you leave a limp silhouette where you
left off—let me be the creature circling
your sleep. I am the most benign unknown;

I do not touch. With what nights are left, plant
your wing beat in my sleep, be the only
hovering thing. If only you could teach me
survival without sustenance, unworried
love, how to find oneself at a window
one morning and think nothing of what happens next.

— Cecily Parks

Fucus vesiculosus.

To make the throw as shown on page 119, enlarge this template by 400%.

LEFT Botanist Anna Atkins placed plant specimens on specially treated paper to create her cyanotypes of British algae, creating vivid blue and white images that evoke silhouettes and stencils.

# BOTANICAL PURSUITS

From women's earliest knowledge of plants' medicinal and culinary qualities to eighteenth- and nineteenth-century amateur botanists' hunger to observe and understand plants of all kinds, women's relationship to plants is complex and fascinating. And when it comes to floral arts, gardens, and other botanical pursuits, countless sources of creative inspiration await.

Women artists of centuries past were celebrated for their depictions of plants—in painting, embroidery, and botanical illustration. Naturalistic depictions of plants became, for some women, a means of taking part in the explosion of interest in the sciences in the seventeenth-century. In the case of the pioneering seventeenth-century German naturalist Maria Sybilla Merian, art became a stepping stone into science and eventually led her to Surinam, where she documented butterfly life stages as well as plant life. More often, however, women incorporated natural plant forms and designs into their creative, domestic pursuits. Floral crafts were immensely popular in the eighteenth-and nineteenth-centuries. Making artificial flowers became tremendously fashionable, and books offered guidance on making them out of fabric, wax, ribbon, beads, and even beetle wings.

When the Linnaean system of plant classification burst onto the scene in the 1760s, it opened up a new path for women interested in botanical pursuits that took them beyond their homes and into the fields. These botanists created collections of mosses and sea plants, documented their observations in drawings and written records, and corresponded with other botanists to share their findings and their questions. The legacy of women's botanical pursuits lives on in illustrations, books, artwork, and correspondence preserved in library collections. It was a nineteenth-century botanist Anna Atkins's landmark work *Photographs of British Algae*, that inspired designer Natalie Chanin to create her Cyanotype Throw (see page 118).

Botanical sources provide visual riches for crafters interested in understanding how historical means of capturing images of flowers and plants can inform new creative pursuits. The following sources will provide more information on the history of women botanists and natural history illustrators:

*Cultivating Women, Cultivating Science: Flora's Daughters at Botany in England, 1760–1860.* Ann B Shtier. Baltimore: Johns Hopkins, 1996.

*The Art of Natural History: Illustrated Treatises and Botanical Paintings, 1400–1850.* Therese O'Mally and Amy R. W. Meyers, eds. Washington: National Gallery of Art, 2008.

*Chrysalis: Maria Sibylla Merian and the Secrets of Metamorphosis.* Kim Todd. Orlando: Harcourt, 2007.

*Ocean Flowers; Impressions from Nature.* Carol Armstrong and Catherine de Zegher, eds. New York: Drawing Center; Princeton: Princeton University Press, 2004.

*Photographs of British Algae*. Anna Atkins. 1843–1853. New York Public Library's digitized copy: http://digitalgallery.nypl.org/nypldigital/explore/dgexplore.cfm?col_id=188

Women and Nature (Memorial Library, University of Wisconsin-Madison): http://specialcollections.library.wisc.edu/exhibits/womennature/index.html

These Library of Congress Subject Headings will lead to more resources on the history of botanical pursuits:

Botanical Illustration.
Plant Prints.
Nature Prints.
Plants in Art.

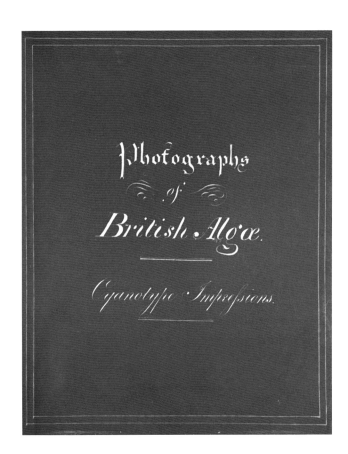

RIGHT When creating her groundbreaking study of British algae, Anna Atkins used the newly discovered cyanotype process (also known as the blueprint process) to create both images of the plants as well as copies of her handwritten text.

# Antiquarian Animal Votive Holders

## DESIGNED BY GRACE BONNEY

ABOUT THE ARTIST
Grace Bonney is
the founder of the
popular design blog
Design*Sponge and the
author of *Design*Sponge
at Home*. She runs the
D*S Biz Ladies Series,
national meetups
for women design
entrepreneurs, as well
as the Design*Sponge
Scholarship, which
supports emerging design
students. She also hosts
a weekly design radio
show, *After the Jump*, on
Heritage Radio Network.
She lives and works in
Brooklyn.

Researchers who study early printed books are often fascinated by the fact that each and every copy they study is different because of the many handcrafted elements involved in making books during the handpress era. From how a book was stitched together to the way illustrations were finished with hand-coloring, small differences make each copy of a work unique. Conrad Gessner's *Historia Animalium*, which writer and animal lover Grace Bonney drew on when creating her votive holders, is no different. Grace examined both an uncolored copy of Gessner's book held in the New York Public Library, as well as the National Library of Medicine's hand-colored copy. In the end, she decided to use the colorful animals. But by simply choosing to draw from a different copy of the same book, the look of the finished product would have been changed.

This project is a quick and easy way to feature favorite animals as they appeared in artwork four centuries ago. With the use of a color printer and a few papercraft supplies, you can turn plain glass candle holders into little monuments of natural history.

BEYOND THE PROJECT:

Gessner's images are full of possibilities. Printed on fabric, the animals could find themselves as bookish blinds, illustrated patchwork, or even individual panels for an animal lover's skirt. Reproduced on paper, the animals could be featured in old-fashioned dioramas, handmade paper lampshades, multimedia collages, pop-up cards, and more. And each page on its own, simply printed and cut into a triangle with its animal front and center, could be strung together to create birthday party bunting that would be perfect for a little one who can't ever get his or her fill of the natural history museum.

To learn about finding other early science and natural history volumes, turn to page 130. And if you're interested in the visual possibilities of early plant illustrations, you'll find out more about how to track down these sources on page 124.

LEFT The peacock is a particularly vivid example of the hand-coloring found in some copies of Gessner's book.

FINISHED DIMENSIONS

- Varied, based on size of candleholders used

SUPPLIES

- Measuring tape
- Clear glass votive candleholders or straight-sided drinking glasses of various sizes
- 8½ × 11" (22 × 28cm) paper, for printing out animal images
- Color printer
- Pencil
- Ruler
- Craft knife
- Cutting mat
- Craft glue
- Rubber band
- Small votive candles (you can use electric candles to be safe)

## STEP 1: MEASURE CANDLEHOLDER

Using a measuring tape, measure candleholder's height and circumference, and add ½" (1.2cm) to circumference. The resulting measurements will be your guide when preparing the antiquarian animal votive cover. The extra ½" (1.2cm) will provide a bit of overlap when wrapping and gluing animal cover around candleholder.

## STEP 2: SELECT AND PREPARE ANIMAL IMAGE

Animal images used here are from Conrad Gessner's *Historia Animalium*. Grace's source was the National Library of Medicine (www.nlm.nih.gov/exhibition/historicalanatomies/gesner_home.html).

Visit the site and download the image of the animal of your choice. Using an image editing program, edit your downloaded image to work with dimensions of your candle holder. Animal's total height from base to top should be approximately ½" to ¾" (1.2 to 2cm) taller than height of your candleholder. As shown in photos, the very top of the peacock's feathers and the rough back of the hedgehog, as well as the rabbit's

ears, goat's horns, and the top of the fox's head, all extend this small amount.

Use a color printer to print out your edited animal.

## STEP 3: MARK CUTTING LINES ON ANIMAL

Use a ruler and pencil to lightly mark a horizontal line along the animal's base, or just slightly below, to create a horizontal baseline.

Measure upward from this horizontal line and mark a second line at a distance equal to height of candleholder. Do not mark across topmost portion of animal image that extends ½" to ¾" (1.2 to 2cm) above this line. This is the portion that will extend above candleholder's rim after you cut out animal.

## STEP 4: CUT OUT ANIMAL

Use a cutting mat and a craft knife to carefully cut along baseline and straight portions of upper line as well. Do not cut off topmost portion of animal image that will extend above candleholder's rim. Next, carefully cut around topmost part of animal image that sticks up above upper line, following details of animal shape as closely as possible.

If you are using very large candleholders, you may need to print out a second animal sheet and attach an additional section to lengthen paper wrapper so it is long enough to wrap around the votive with a ½" (1.2cm) overlap. Using text sections from the book images to lengthen the paper wrapper provides a literary touch.

## STEP 5: SECURE WRAPPER AROUND CANDLEHOLDER

Wrap paper animal cover around candleholder's exterior, securing it with a bit of glue. Place a rubber band loosely around candleholder to keep paper secure while glue dries. When glue is dry, remove rubber band and place a candle or electric candle in holder.

# ILLUSTRATED ANIMALS AND NATURAL HISTORY

When sixteenth-century Swiss scholar Conrad Gessner began his monumental book *Historia Animalium*, he succeeded in creating a work that would become a foundational text of modern zoology, as well as one that would continue to attract readers and browsers today. That book, and many other early natural history works depicting the animal world, offer graphic inspiration along with a view into the world of Renaissance science, zoology, and art.

Gessner was trained as a botanist, linguist, and physician, and was a voracious reader of early science works that came before him. In *Historia Animalium*, printed in five large folio volumes, he attempted to describe the entirety of the animal kingdom, including birds, fish, mammals, and even fantastical creatures like sea monsters, many-headed hydras, and unicorns. He included vast numbers of woodcut illustrations by a variety of artists, including Albrecht Dürer, that continue to fascinate and draw in scholars.

Gessner died in his library, among his books and collections, when the plague swept through Zurich in 1565. But his achievement in the form of *Historia Animalium* and his many other works live on in libraries worldwide. When designer Grace Bonney went in search of antiquarian animals for her votive holders (see page 126), she turned to the digitized copy of Gessner's book held at the National Library of Medicine.

Here are some places where you can browse a variety of early natural history illustrations as well as historical images of natural history museum exhibitions:

Biodiversity Heritage Library, a consortium of natural history and botanical libraries: www.biodiversitylibrary.org

Historical Anatomies: National Library of Medicine: www.nlm.nih.gov/exhibition/historicalanatomies/gesner_home.html

Wellcome Library: http://images.wellcome.ac.uk

Royal Society Picture Library: https://pictures.royalsociety.org/about

Picturing the Museum (American Museum of Natural History Research Library): http://images.library.amnh.org/photos/index.html

These books offer more glimpses of early natural history illustrations:

*Art and Nature: Three Centuries of Natural History Art from Around the World.* Judith Magee. Vancouver: Greystone Books, 2009.

*Beasts and Bestiaries: The Representation of Animals from Prehistory to the Renaissance.* Francesco Mezzalira. Turin: U. Allemandi, 2001.

*Prints and the Pursuit of Knowledge in Early Modern Europe.* Susan Dackerman, ed. Cambridge: Harvard Art Museums; New Haven: Distributed by Yale University Press, 2011.

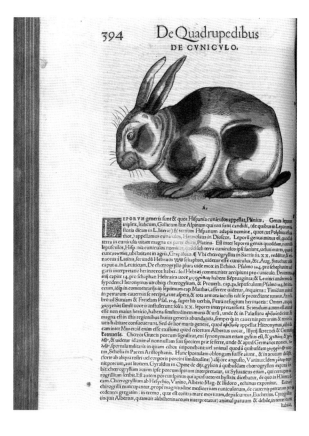

These Library of Congress Subject Headings will lead to more early natural history resources:

> ANIMALS IN ART.
>
> CABINETS OF CURIOSITIES — HISTORY.
>
> COLLECTORS AND COLLECTING —
>
>         HISTORY.
>
> NATURE IN ART.
>
> NATURAL HISTORY ILLUSTRATION.
>
> NATURAL HISTORY ILLUSTRATORS.
>
> ZOOLOGY — EARLY WORKS TO 1800.
>
> ZOOLOGY — PRE-LINNEAN WORKS.

If you're interested in early illustrations of plants as well, visit page 124 for more research ideas.

ABOVE Gessner attempted to document and organize the entire world's animal life, from the largest creatures like elephants to the smallest, such as rabbits and birds.

# Soil Profile Growth Chart

## DESIGNED BY LIESL GIBSON

ABOUT THE ARTIST

Since 2008, Liesl Gibson has designed and launched a series of pattern brands for home sewists, as well as lines of fabric to accompany her patterns. Her brands include Oliver + S (children's clothing), Lisette (women's clothing), and Straight Stitch Society (gifts and accessories). She is also the author of *Oliver + S Little Things to Sew*. In 2010, Liesl was given the FabShop Network's Rising Star Award, an honor bestowed by independent fabric store owners across North America. Liesl lives in Manhattan. You can find out more about her designs at www.lieslandco.com.

When it came to selecting a research topic for a handmade project for this book, Liesl Gibson recalled the soil profile charts her father, a soil scientist, showed her as a child. With their views deep into the ground revealing various soil layers, and the different sedimentary layers represented by contrasting textures and colors, these research diagrams provided her with unexpected visual inspiration. For this project, specifically, an illustration on the spine of an iconic nineteenth-century geology textbook, *Elements of Geology: A Text-Book for Colleges and for the General Reader*, by Joseph LeConte, caught her eye.

Liesl's soil profile growth chart is a recognizable visual nod to her rich geological source materials, but it doesn't take itself too seriously. It's a quick and fun project to make, and involves only a small amount of sewing but has plenty of room for improvising.

BEYOND THIS PROJECT:

What makes the structure of Liesl's growth chart interesting is how it lends itself to being constructed through the years as your child grows up, just as soil and rock build up in layers over time. Instead of making it all at once, consider the option of incorporating bits of fabric from your son or daughter's outgrown clothes (or scraps left over from clothes you've made for him or her) over time, to add a bit of nostalgia to the project.

If you are not a fan of embroidery, remember that you can record your child's growth marks with a fine fabric pen instead. Just be sure to follow the manufacturer's instructions on the fabric pen to ensure that the marks will remain permanent.

If you'd rather not sew the project but are fond of working with paper, the soil profile growth chart could be constructed as a collage using a variety of papers on a sturdy cardstock scroll base instead.

If you're interested in learning more about the world of resources related to soil profiles and geology, see page 139 for ideas on getting started.

- 57 × 12" (145 × 30cm)

## SUPPLIES

- One 25 × 60" (64 × 152cm) rectangle natural linen
- Sewing machine (with optional walking foot)
- Thread, in a color to match linen
- Iron and ironing board
- Straight pins
- Tailor's chalk
- Ruler
- Fabric scissors
- 1 yard (91cm) fusible webbing (and parchment paper, if required by manufacturer's instructions)
- Twenty 8" (20cm)-wide fabric scraps, 4 to 8" (10 to 20cm) tall, in various colors and patterns, for the soil layers
- Four 3 × 2" (8 × 5cm) green fabric scraps, for leaves
- Fabric scissors
- Dark brown thread
- One 60" (152cm) vinyl or fabric measuring tape
- Thread, in a color to match measuring tape
- Two ⅜" (1cm)-diameter by 14" (36cm)-long dowel rods
- Wood stain and brush (optional)
- 24" (60cm) ribbon or string for hanging chart (optional)
- Dark brown pearl cotton embroidery thread and a hand-sewing needle or permanent fabric-marking pen

## STEP 1: PREPARE BACKGROUND LINEN

Fold linen in half lengthwise, with two long edges together and right sides facing. Use a sewing machine and leaving a ½" (1.2cm) seam allowance, sew two long edges together. Iron seam allowance.

Turn linen tube right side out and iron flat so seam is positioned along left edge of rectangle. Pin the two layers of fabric together at various points to prevent them from shifting.

Use zigzag stitch on sewing machine to sew through both layers of fabric at one short end of rectangle, placing line of stitches close to raw edges, to finish edge. Repeat to finish raw edges on other short end.

## STEP 2: CREATE DOWEL CASINGS

Place linen rectangle on work surface, with long side seam on left side. The side of rectangle facing up will be front (right side) of growth chart. Use tailor's chalk and a ruler to draw a line 1¼" (3mm) from finished edge of top short end. Draw a second line 2" (5cm) from finished edge.

Fold fabric to wrong side along first line you drew. Machine-stitch folded layers together along second line. This will make a casing for dowel at top of growth chart.

Repeat these steps at bottom short end to make second dowel casing.

## STEP 3: PREPARE SOIL LAYERS

Cut a piece of fusible web to be just slightly smaller than one of your soil layer fabric scraps (cutting the web slightly smaller than the fabric prevents fusible web from sticking out over edges and fusing to your iron as you work).

Following manufacturer's instructions, fuse web to wrong side of soil layer fabric scrap.

Trim scrap so that it is 7" (18cm) wide. Be sure edge of fused web extends all the way to right and left edges of fabric scrap after trimming. (Top and bottom of each piece will be trimmed in next step so leave them varied.)

Repeat these steps with each soil layer fabric scrap, until each one is backed with fusible web and trimmed to 7" (18cm) wide (with varied heights).

## STEP 4: MARK GROWTH CHART FOR SOIL LAYER PLACEMENT

Place growth chart on work surface, with right side up and long side seam along left side. Use tailor's chalk and a ruler to draw four lines on front of growth chart: one vertical line ¾" (2cm) in from long left edge; one vertical line 2½" (6cm) in from long right edge; one horizontal line 2½" (6cm) up from bottom casing edge; and one horizontal line 7" (18cm) down from top casing edge. Vertical lines should span length of chart and horizontal lines should span its width.

These lines will act as guides for positioning the various items on growth chart.

### STEP 5: ADD SOIL LAYERS

Soil layers will be added from bottom up. Gather soil layers prepared in Step 3 and select one to be bottom layer.

Trim bottom edge of selected soil layer so it is straight and square to two trimmed side edges, making sure edge of fused web extends all the way to bottom edge of fabric scrap after trimming.

Position fabric scrap, right side up, on growth chart so bottom and left edges match chalk lines you drew. Following manufacturer's instructions, fuse fabric scrap in place.

Using dark brown thread and a straight sewing stitch, machine-stitch sides and bottom edge of fused fabric approximately ¹/₈" (3mm) from cut edges of fabric. This will help to define edge and secure fabric.

Select a second fabric scrap for next layer of soil. Trim its bottom edge with a slight curve to mimic unevenness of a soil layer. Again, be sure fused web extends all the way to edge after trimming. Trim its top edge to be slightly taller than you want the finished soil layer to be.

Position second fabric scrap on top of first soil layer so it completely overlaps top edge of first layer. Fuse and edgestitch fabric on sides and bottom edge as you did with first layer.

Continue to work your way up growth chart, adding soil layers as you go. If desired, you can make some layers taller than others, and you can vary curves and angles of soil layers, as shown in photograph.

You can complete growth chart all at once, or you can add layers over time so layers grow with your child.

Stop adding fabric layers when your soil layers reach top chalk line. Edgestitch all four sides of top fabric layer to finish it.

### STEP 6: ADD PLANTS

Cut pieces of fusible web just slightly smaller than green fabric scraps you will use for leaf. Following manufacturer's instructions, fuse web to wrong side of leaf fabric scraps.

Use template on page 137 to cut leaves from web-backed leaf scraps. Following manufacturer's instructions and using finished photograph on page 133 as a guide to placement, fuse leaves approximately 1½" (4cm) from top edge of top soil layer.

Stitch plant stems and roots, either making up your own stem and roots by stitching freehand or by following lines on templates.

### STEP 7: ADD MEASURING TAPE

Use scissors to cut ends off measuring tape, trimming below 12" (30cm) mark and above 60" (152cm) mark on tape. Just inside long vertical chalk line along long right edge of growth chart, align tape with 12" (30cm) mark near bottom of soil layers and 60" (152cm) mark at top. Pin or tape measuring tape in place.

Lengthen sewing machine stitch length to approximately 3.5mm and edgestitch tape to growth chart using thread to match measuring tape. (If you have a walking foot, it would be useful for this step.) Most measuring tapes are pliable enough that you can just stitch through them without any problem. But take care, as you stitch, that you keep tape lying smoothly against fabric so neither tape nor fabric layers get stretched or distorted.

### STEP 8: ADD DOWELS AND HANG CHART

Stain dowels, if desired, according to instructions on stain.

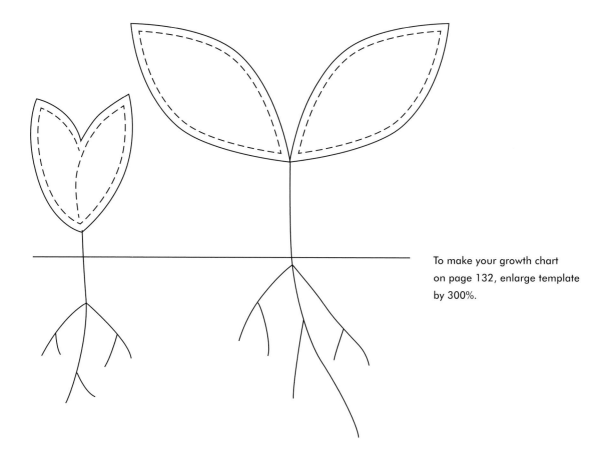

To make your growth chart on page 132, enlarge template by 300%.

When dry, feed one dowel through top casing and one through bottom.

Decide how you want to hang chart: Either tie one end of a 24" (61cm) piece of ribbon or string to each end of top dowel and hang growth chart from a nail, or position a nail under each end of the dowel and rest dowel on nails (this method will keep the chart more steady).

Whichever way you choose, take care to position chart so that 12" (30cm) mark on measuring tape is exactly 12" (30cm) from floor.

**STEP 9: RECORD CHILD'S GROWTH**
If you're using embroidery to mark your child's growth, use tailor's chalk to mark child's height at right edge of growth chart and write date near each height marking. Then use brown pearl cotton to embroider over lines you drew with a simple backstitch.

If you prefer to use a fabric pen, mark height along right edge of the chart, add the date, and be sure to follow manufac-turer's instructions for making the markings permanent.

| | | | |
|---|---|---|---|
| Psychozoic. | | Recent. Quaternary. | Tapir, Peccary, Bison, Llama. *Megatherium, Mylodon, Elephas.* |
| Cenozoic. | Tertiary. | Pliocene. | Pliohippus Beds. *Pliohippus, Mastodon, Bos, etc.* |
| | | Miocene. | Miohippus Beds. *Miohippus, Diceratherium, Thinohyus.* Oreodon Beds. *Edentates, Hyænodon, Hyracodon.* Brontotherium Beds. *Mesohippus, Menodus, Elotherium.* |
| | | Eocene. | Diplacodon Beds. *Epihippus, Amynodon.* Dinoceras Beds. *Tinoceras, Uintatherium, Limnohyus, Orohippus, Helaletes, Colonoceras.* Coryphodon Beds. *Eohippus, Monkeys, Carnivores, Ungulates, Tillodonts, Rodents, Serpents.* |
| Mesozoic. | Cretaceous. | | Laramie Series. *Triceratops.* Upper Cretaceous of N. J. *Hadrosaurus, Dryptosaurus.* Pteranodon Beds. *Birds with Teeth, Hesperornis, Ichthyornis,* Mosasaurs, Pterodactyls, Plesiosaurs. Dakota Group. Comanche Group. |
| | Jurassic. | | Atlantosaurus Beds. *Dinosaurs, Apatosaurus, Allosaurus, Nanosaurus.* Turtles. *Diplodocus.* |
| | Triassic. | | Connecticut River Beds. First Mammals (Marsupials), (*Dromatherium*). Dinosaur Footprints, *Amphisaurus,* Crocodiles (*Belodon*). |
| Palæozoic. | Carboniferous. | | Permian. First Reptiles. Coal-Measures. Subcarboniferous. First known Amphibians (Labyrinthodonts). |
| | Devonian. | | Corniferous. Schoharie Grit. First Fish Fauna. |
| | Silurian. | | Upper Silurian. / Lower Silurian. — No Vertebrates except in the Uppermost Part. |
| | Cambrian. | | Primordial. |
| Archæan. | Archæan. | | Huronian. / Laurentian. — No Distinct Organic Remains. |

Fig. 255.—Section of the Earth's Crust, to illustrate Vertebrate Life in America. (Slightly modified from Marsh.)

the several epochs and periods of the history of the earth in the inverse order of their occurrence. Commencing with a thorough discussion of "*causes now in operation*," i. e., geological history of the present time, as that which is best known, they make this the basis for the study of the epoch immediately preceding, and which, therefore, is most like it. Having acquired a knowledge of this, the student passes to the preceding, and so on. This has the great advantage of passing ever from the better known to the less known, which is the order of induction. Other geologists prefer to follow the natural order of events. This has the great advantage of bringing out the philosophy of the history—the law of evolution. The first method is the best method of *investigation;* the second method is the best method of *presentation.*

As in human history, so in the geological history, the recorded events of the earliest times are very few and meager, but become more and more numerous and interesting as we approach the present time. Our account of the Archæan era will, there-

fore, be quite ⟨...⟩
though this era⟨...⟩
scription of th⟨...⟩
next even into⟨...⟩

**Prehistoric**⟨...⟩
fect records of⟨...⟩
an infinite aby⟨...⟩
strictly to geol⟨...⟩
not by *written*⟨...⟩
scientific reaso⟨...⟩
est system of r⟨...⟩

## LAUREN⟨...⟩

IT is one ⟨...⟩
lished this as a⟨...⟩

It had bee⟨...⟩
there still exi⟨...⟩
and apparentl⟨...⟩
as lowermost ⟨...⟩
zoic volume.⟨...⟩
Logan, reveale⟨...⟩
torted, metam⟨...⟩
*ing Primordia⟨...⟩*
relation not c⟨...⟩
in Nebraska, ⟨...⟩
Texas, New M⟨...⟩
try, for the sa⟨...⟩
on the west co⟨...⟩
and an unde⟨...⟩
of Canada. S⟨...⟩
been found u⟨...⟩
and Bavaria, ⟨...⟩
shows great a⟨...⟩
time, and the⟨...⟩
no longer any ⟨...⟩
system.⟨...⟩

The follo⟨...⟩
Palæozoic an⟨...⟩
Scotland.

# SOIL PROFILES

Just as you might study a person's face in profile—looking at how the forehead, nose, mouth, and chin all stack up to form the whole thing—a soil scientist studies soil profiles. A soil profile is a vertical cross-section of a particular area of soil, from topsoil to bottom. In between are what scientists call soil horizons: horizontal stripes showing how the soil's composition changes as it gets nearer to or farther from the surface.

To understand a soil profile is to know its soil horizons. And before the ease of capturing visual data by photograph and reproducing it easily for publication, soil profiles were reproduced as drawings, with each soil horizon depicted as a different textural graphic pattern. It was soil profiles like these that inspired designer Liesl Gibson of Oliver + S to create her layered fabric growth chart (see page 132).

If you'd like to learn more about the history of taking soil surveys and making soil profiles, the 1951 *Soil Survey Manual* provides an interesting place to start and even discusses the importance of color in soil profiles. It has been digitized and is available online at the U.S. Department of Agriculture's National Agriculture Library at naldc.nal.usda.gov/download/CAT10663496/PDF.

Today, soil profiles might be captured as photographs of the striping soil horizons, complete with measuring tape draped along the profile's face. The U.S. Department of Agriculture's Natural Resources Conservation Service posts images of soil profiles like this from the field at soils.usda.gov/gallery/photos/profiles.

Rocks and geology often receive similar graphic treatment in publications, and "geologic cross-sections," "geologic columns," and "stratigraphic columns" are keyword searches worth trying if you are searching specifically for geological cross-section diagrams.

If you'd like to learn more about soils and rocks, try these Subject Heading searches:

> MINERALOGY.
> SEDIMENTARY ROCKS.
> SOIL PROFILES.
> SOIL PROFILES — HANDBOOKS, MANUALS, ETC.
> SOIL SURVEYS.
> SOILS.
> SOILS — HANDBOOKS, MANUALS, ETC.

LEFT Geologist Joseph LeConte was a friend of naturalist John Muir and an early leader of the Sierra Club, and the Yosemite National Park library building bears his name. Pictured here is his iconic text, *Elements of Geology* (New York: Appleton, 1891).

# Wool Rose Fascinator

## DESIGNED BY GRETCHEN HIRSCH

ABOUT THE ARTIST

Gretchen Hirsch writes, designs home sewing patterns, and teaches sewing. She is the author of *Gertie's New Book for Better Sewing: A Modern Guide to Couture-Style Sewing Using Basic Vintage Techniques*. She lives in Beacon, New York, and you'll find her online at blogforbettersewing .com.

ABOVE

Redouté's *Les Roses* provides floral inspiration.

When sewing teacher and designer Gretchen Hirsch started considering ideas for her library research, her top-priority subjects were hats and roses. The New York Public Library has plenty of materials on both of these topics, so I helped her to identify some sources to get her started.

To provide her with color inspiration in the world of roses, I shared with her one of my favorite illustrated works on flowers: Pierre Joseph Redouté's *Les Roses* (1817–1824). This work contains 170 hand-finished engravings, beautiful color prints of nearly every rose known to exist at that time. And to address Gretchen's questions about hat fashions, I suggested a number of millinery magazines from the first half of the twentieth century, as well as a few books that took hat-making in a bit of a quirky DIY direction (her favorite: *It's Fun to Make a Hat* by Helene Garnell [1944]). After working her way through a few dozen volumes, she came away with plenty of source photographs for her later reference, as well as a plan for her fascinator covered with wool blossoms in colors inspired by the rich hues of Redouté's roses.

The technique of making these wool roses is straightforward. It requires just cutting, arranging, and gluing wool felt strips. But the resulting cluster of vivid petals is much more than the sum of its parts.

BEYOND THIS PROJECT:

Simply by varying the number, size, and arrangement of the blooms, you can make your own customized fascinator. You could also, instead of adding a hair clip to the back, attach a pin back and create a glamorous brooch or embellishment to add to a hat. And if you'd like more color inspiration drawn from Redouté's prints, you can see all of his roses at the New York Public Library's website.

To learn more about millinery magazines, check out the suggested sources on page 144. For a different take on artificial flowers, see page 146. And to learn more about botanical research, turn to page 124.

COMING ATTRACTION

ABOVE  Rosa Gallica (*Purpurea velutina, parva*) by Redouté.

FINISHED DIMENSIONS

- 3 × 5" (8 × 13cm)

SUPPLIES

- Three pieces wool felt, each at least 6 × 18" (15 × 46cm), in salmon, coral, and bright pink
- Ruler
- Fabric scissors
- Hot glue gun
- One 2 × 4" (5 × 10cm) piece of heavy craft interfacing (sew-in, not fusible)
- One 1¾" (4.5cm) metal alligator hair clip with teeth
- Chalk pencil or other marking tool

### STEP 1: CUT FELT INTO STRIPS

The fascinator is made of 1 large rose, 2 medium roses, and 1 small one. Measure and cut felt as follows for strips needed to create 4 roses:

· For large rose: Two $^{7}/_{8}$ × 18" (22mm × 46cm) strips bright pink felt

· For first medium rose: One $^{7}/_{8}$ × 18" (22mm × 46cm) strip coral felt

· For second medium rose: One $^{7}/_{8}$ × 18" (22mm × 46cm) strip salmon felt

· For small rose: One $^{5}/_{8}$ × 13" (1.5 × 33cm) strip coral felt

### STEP 2: FORM LARGE ROSE

Begin by rolling one end of first felt strip tightly into a coil to create rose center (illustration A). When center measures approximately $^{3}/_{8}$" (1cm) across, begin to twist felt strip away from center as you continue to coil felt strip around center (illustration B). Use hot glue gun to place a drop or two of hot glue between the rose folds regularly as you work, to secure your felt coil (illustration C). When you complete coiling first strip, begin coiling second one, overlapping two ends and gluing them in place (illustration D).

### STEP 3: FORM MEDIUM AND SMALL ROSES

The 2 medium and 1 small roses are made

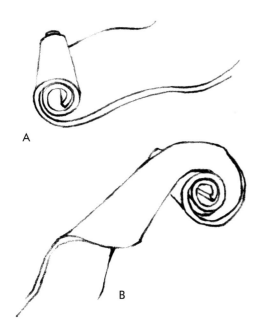

A

B

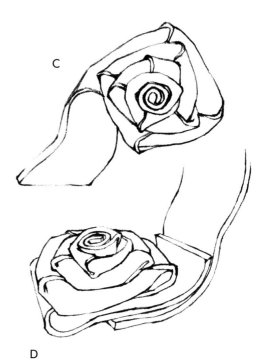

C

D

using the same basic technique, but the center is slightly smaller and only a single felt strip is used to make each.

For medium and small roses, when center measures approximately ¼" (5mm) across, begin to twist felt strip away from center as you continue to coil felt strip around center (illustration E).

### STEP 4: MAKE FASCINATOR BASE
On craft interfacing, draw an oval with gently pointed ends measuring 4½" long and 2" (5cm) wide. Cut out this shape. Using oval of interfacing as guide, cut a piece of felt in color of choice in same shape. Hot-glue felt to craft interfacing.

### STEP 5: ATTACH ROSES TO BASE
Arrange 4 roses on base as desired, using photo as guide, and use hot glue gun to glue in place.

### STEP 6: ATTACH HAIR CLIP
Turn over fascinator so it is face down on work surface. Use hot glue gun to attach hair clip to center back of fascinator (illustration F). Allow glue to dry before wearing.

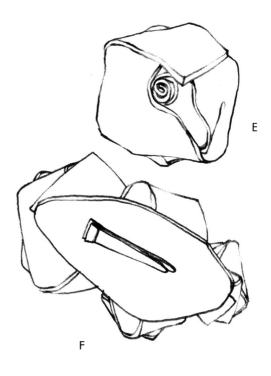

E

F

# MILLINERY ARTS

In the nineteenth and early twentieth centuries, millinery styles—like most fashions—originated in Paris and London and traveled to the United States by way of finished hats as well as publications about the latest designs. From wide-brimmed straw hats to fantastical feathered creations to close-fitting felt cloches, new designs were copied by skilled millinery artists and adapted for regional tastes.

The printed sources from which some millinery artists drew their inspiration now live on in the collections of some research libraries. From manuals on how to make artificial flowers (an important skill for milliners as far back as the eighteenth-century) to trade magazines for professional milliners, these publications reveal an art, a profession, and a highly specialized handmaking skill. And beyond professional periodicals, fashion magazines in general can offer a goldmine of visual information on past decades' styles as well.

If you're interested in the fashions of hats, in particular times and places, an ideal source of inspiration will be millinery and hairdressing magazines published during the era that interests you. And research libraries, with their dedicated interest in collecting and preserving long runs of magazines and periodicals, are the perfect place to hunt for mountains of vintage visuals. You can start by finding out what magazines might cover the fashion topic that interests you, and then identify the ones that were published during the time period you want to explore. For example, when designer Gretchen Hirsch came to the New York Public Library in search of post–World War II millinery styles, she found issues of *British Millinery* from the late 1940s and early 1950s to offer the perfect inspiration (see her project on page 140).

Here are a few periodicals from the first half of the twentieth century that can provide millinery inspiration.

*Illustrated Milliner*. New York: The Illustrated Milliner Co., 1900–1934.

*Chapeaux Modernes*. Paris: G. Lyon, 1934–40.

*British Millinery*. London: United Trade Press for the Proprietors, British Hat Trade Publications, 1940s–50s.

*Millinery Monitor*. New York: Seymour Mittelmark, Inc., 1937–1947.

*The Designer*. New York: Standard Fashion Company, 1898–1920.

Because the work of designing hats depends very much on the related work of hair design, illustrations in hairstyle publications can offer some related inspiration and information as well. They are worth checking out when considering how vintage-style hair arrangements can work with vintage-style hats and other accessories. Here are a couple of titles worth paging through:

*Modern Hairdressing and Beauty Culture*. Toronto: Mines and Metals Publishers, 1927–1943.

*The American Hairdresser*. Columbus, Ohio: National Hairdressers and Cosmetologists Association, 1904–1971.

You could use these Subject Headings to track down more sources on hats as well as hairdressing:

MILLINERY.
MILLINERY — PERIODICALS.
HATS.
HAIRDRESSING — PERIODICALS.
WOMEN'S HATS.

*Evening Head-dress, representing a beautiful Wreath.*—The hair is banded in front, and twisted at the back part of the head; but it may be arranged in any style which taste may suggest. The wreath is composed of the delicate azalia, with its light-green lustrous foliage faithfully copied from nature; and the petals of the flowers beautifully frosted to represent dew. The wreath is mounted in the Italian style, now so fashionable; having full bouquets at each side, and a narrow row of foliage and buds in the middle. It should be placed on the head with the top forward on the forehead, as shown in the engraving.

ABOVE Advice about hats and hairstyles can be found in many historical women's periodicals. This illustration, from the November 1849 *Godey's Lady's Book*, describes a wreathlike hair ornament to be worn "in the Italian style."

# Felt Dogwood Blossoms

## DESIGNED BY JESSICA PIGZA

June Number—Just Out

GODEY'S

JUNE
1896 MAGAZINE

10 Cents a Copy    One Dollar a Year

ABOVE *Godey's Lady's Book* often included instructions for making artificial flowers for embellishing anything from desk accessories and candle holders to clothing and hair.

While assisting a library visitor with a search of nineteenth-century women's periodicals that included *Godey's Lady's Book and Magazine* and *Ingalls' Home and Art Magazine*, I was struck by how often artificial flowers appeared. There were instructions for creating flowers out of leather, fabric, or wax, and their means of construction were complicated, time-consuming, and surely toxic in some cases. I wasn't about to start crimping silk with hot irons or applying acid to leaves, but I did start reading more about the use of these fake flowers in fashion and home décor. And soon enough I was playing with fabric and felt at home, making flowers of my own.

Serendipity struck again a few weeks later, as I paged through François André Michaux's *The North American Sylva* (1841) and became interested in the flowering dogwood called *Cornus florida*. Each blossom of this tree is made up of four bracts, which look like large white petals, surrounded by yellow-green flower clusters. In Michaux's book I learned that dogwood bark can be used to make ink. And in *Vegetable Materia Medica of the United States; or, Medical Botany* (1818–1825), the bark of the tree is cited for its usefulness in dental hygiene. Regardless of its uses in the past, the dogwood remains a sign of spring's arrival, and I hope this project makes you think of that hopeful season.

BEYOND THIS PROJECT:

I've provided patterns for two sizes of blossoms, but you can make any size you want by enlarging or reducing the patterns. I like the idea of clustering a handful of different sizes along the neckline of a dress for a fancy night out.

You might also experiment with adapting the basic shaping techniques and using different colors and shapes to create other flowers.

To learn more about finding handmade project ideas in historical women's magazines, see page 150. If you're interested in finding out more about women's botanical pursuits in the nineteenth century, turn to page 124. And for a different and very glamorous take on fabric flowers, see Gretchen Hirsch's rose fascinator on page 140.

SMALL BLOSSOM: 1⅞" (4.8cm) diameter

LARGE BLOSSOM: 2⅞" (7.3cm) diameter

SUPPLIES

- Paper scissors
- Straight pins
- One 6" (15cm) piece thick white or ivory felt
- Fabric scissors
- Thread, in color to match felt
- Hand-sewing needle
- Two ¾" (2cm)-diameter green craft pom-poms
- 1 skein brown embroidery floss

## STEP 1: CREATE FLOWER PATTERNS

Photocopy the two flower templates on page 149 at 100% and cut them out. Dotted lines in each template indicate where to stitch in Steps 3 and 4—these markings do not need to be transferred to felt.

## STEP 2: CUT OUT FELT IN FLOWER SHAPES

Pin two flower templates side by side on felt. Cut around templates to form two felt flower shapes. Set patterns aside.

## STEP 3: CINCH CENTER

Choose one side of felt flower shape to be front.

Using dotted line on large template at right as a guide, use two strands of all-purpose thread to stitch a running stitch in a circle at center of flower shape, beginning and ending stitches at back of felt. Gently cinch thread so felt is gathered together just a bit, and use your fingertip to nudge center-front of flower shape gently so that it forms a depression. Knot off thread in back.

## STEP 4: CREATE CURVED BRACTS

Using dotted line of small template at right as a guide, use a single strand of all-purpose thread to place an invisible row of shallow running stitches ⅛" (3mm) from each bract edge as follows:

Starting on back side, slide needle tip partway into felt (but not all the way through to front). Then, bring needle tip out on back again near where it entered. Make following stitch next to this one, and continue all around one bract, creating invisible shallow running stitches. As you complete each bract, gently cinch thread to create a slight curve or cup shape in bract. Then begin next bract.

Knot off thread on back of fabric after all four bracts are stitched, cinched, and curved.

## STEP 5: ADD GREEN POM-POM CENTER

Using a single strand of thread, sew a pom-pom to center front of flower. Attach pom-pom securely by sewing through felt flower center, sewing through pom-pom core, and then back through felt flower center twice. Knot off on back.

If you'd like to make center of smaller dogwood slightly smaller, use scissors to trim pom-pom all around until it is the size you wish. The small dogwood pom-pom pictured on page 147 has been trimmed from ¾" (2cm) to ½" (1.2cm) in diameter.

## STEP 6: ADD BROWN BRACT TIPS

Using a single strand of brown embroidery floss and using photo as your guide, add a series of small stitches to notch at center of each bract edge. Wrap stitches around from back to front, adding 4 stitches to each bract of small dogwood blossom, and 6 to each bract of large blossom.

Begin and end on back of flower to hide knots.

RIGHT The dogwood specimen pictured here was published in 1841 in *The North American Sylva* by François André Michaux, who collected a variety of plants and trees while traveling in North America and brought the specimens home to France.

SMALL BLOSSOM

LARGE BLOSSOM

# EARLY WOMEN'S MAGAZINES

The first American magazine to target women readers directly was launched as early as 1792, with the publication of *The Lady's Magazine and Repository of Entertaining Knowledge*. Promising to "inspire the female mind with a love of religion, patience, prudence, and fortitude," this literary magazine was the start of a publishing niche that eventually grew to include *Godey's Lady's Book and Magazine* and other nineteenth-century standards for female audiences. These early publications, though all quite different in many ways, laid the groundwork for the runaway successes that would come to dominate women's magazines a generation later.

McCall's, *Ladies' Home Journal*, *Woman's Home Companion*, *Delineator*, *Good Housekeeping*, and *Pictorial Review* became media giants of the late nineteenth- and early twentieth-centuries. Together they earned the title "Big Six" because their unprecedented subscription and readership levels towered over those of any other magazine genre of the time. These women's magazines offered a mix of literary content alongside advice on housekeeping, domestic economy, cooking, and sewing. And three of these—*Delineator*, *McCall's*, and *Pictorial Review*—were also filled with illustrations promoting home sewing projects as well, since these magazines were owned by pattern companies and used explicitly as a way to promote sales of their brands.

What all this means for curious sewists and designers today is that these magazines are a rich resource for both information and ideas. With their attention to the home sewing culture of the late-nineteenth and early-twentieth century, their evocative period advertisements, and their reader-driven features on homemaking questions, cooking solutions, and handicraft ideas—submitted by the readers themselves—early women's magazines are a fascinating window into everyday history and a means of glimpsing what many women read, took an interest in, and made for themselves during that period.

From embroidery patterns and dressmaking illustrations to guides to fancy napkin folding and instructions for making soft toys or home goods, these magazines offer lots of kernels of ideas. After browsing through a number of issues of *Godey's Lady's Book and Magazine* and *Ingalls' Home and Art Magazine*, and being drawn into their regular features on making artificial flowers, I was inspired to create dogwood flowers out of felt (see page 146).

Here are two books to get you started if you'd like to read more about the history of women's magazines:

*A History of Popular Women's Magazines in the United States, 1792–1995.* Mary Ellen Zuckerman. Westport, Connecticut: Greenwood Press, 1998.

*The Adman in the Parlor: Magazines and the Gendering of Consumer Culture, 1880s to 1910s.* Ellen Gruber Garvey. New York: Oxford, 1996.

To track down women's magazines and periodicals in your area research library, you can search directly in your library catalog for the magazine titles mentioned above. You might also use these Subject Headings to discover other titles:

HOME ECONOMICS — PERIODICALS.
DRESSMAKING — PERIODICALS.
NEEDLEWORK — PERIODICALS.
WOMEN'S PERIODICALS.

RIGHT *Pictorial Review* featured enticing illustrations of dress patterns available for purchase for home sewing. The January 1916 issue glimpsed here depicts a number of dresses, including a "semiprincess costume" and a dramatically draped skirt in plaid.

# Cartouche Embroidery

## DESIGNED BY REBECCA RINGQUIST

ABOUT THE ARTIST
Rebecca Ringquist is a Brooklyn-based visual artist who creates drawings on paper and stitched drawings on fabric. She teaches nationally and has led workshops at Squam and at Haystack Mountain School of Crafts. You'll find her online at http://drop-cloth.blogspot.com.

When Rebecca Ringquist visited the New York Public Library's Map Division, she was drawn to the historical maps she studied. She found it fascinating that cartouches contained all kinds of information in an ornate decorative format, from inside jokes and pseudonyms to dates and purposeful mistakes.

Rebecca's project interprets these traditional ornamental features in linen, floss, and handwritten messages. As a personalized label, it makes a perfect addition to a handmade quilt, but you can make and use the design on other kinds of personalized gifts and handmade projects as well.

Rebecca designed the cartouche to enable you to add an extra personal touch by using your own handwriting. If you aren't crazy about your handwriting, however, you can get some guidance elsewhere on your lettering. For example, try printing the letters and words you want in the size you wish using a word processing program, and trace them using the same Sulky Solvy technique described below. You might also, of course, go hunting for letter designs in library collections. Rebecca especially likes looking at the letters used in children's books for inspiration. Be sure to see pages 80 and 88 for tips on researching letters and alphabets. Soon enough, you just might be designing your own hand-embroidered alphabet.

BEYOND THIS PROJECT:

While the idea for Rebecca's cartouche initially took root as a quilt label, it can be used in other ways as well. Just think of it as a unique tag for labeling your handmade projects and gifts. It could be added to handmade garments, cloth book covers, and more. Or, you might add a cartouche to a nicely hemmed piece of linen and use it to wrap a special gift for a friend (who can then keep the stitched linen artwork as a special hand towel or dresser scarf).

And of course, you can search libraries' historical map collections for ideas on how to design your own personal cartouche. See page 156 for research ideas.

ABOVE Elaborately decorated cartouches like this one, on a 1736 map of English North America, caught Rebecca's eye while examining historical maps.

ABOVE To create the embroidery pictured here, photocopy and enlarge or reduce the template above as you prefer.

RIGHT: In this detail you can see Rebecca's floss color choices; you can use this as a guide to your own color choices or create your own palette.

- Finished embroidery: 7" (18cm) wide × 5" (13cm) tall

## SUPPLIES

- Blue painter's tape
- Pencil
- Ultrafine permanent marker in contrasting color to fabric
- One 10 × 8" (25 × 20cm) piece Sulky Solvy water-soluble stabilizer, Original Weight
- Iron and ironing board
- 13 × 12" (33 × 30cm) piece pale green linen or cotton fabric
- Embroidery hoop
- Embroidery floss, in colors of your choice
- Hand-sewing needle (a size 5 embroidery needle works well)

## STEP 1: PREPARE EMBROIDERY TEMPLATE

Photocopy template on page 154, enlarging or reducing it as you prefer. Use blue painter's tape to tape template face up on your work surface.

Sketch the personal name details and numbers for year onto template in pencil. When satisfied, go over them with ultrafine permanent marker. (See the suggestions on page 152 if you prefer not to add these details in your own handwriting.)

## STEP 2: TRANSFER EMBROIDERY PATTERN TO SULKY SOLVY

Place a piece of Sulky Solvy over template, centering pattern underneath. Tape edges of Sulky Solvy to your work surface with painter's tape.

Using ultrafine permanent marker, trace all template's lines and details onto Sulky Solvy.

Gently peel Sulky Solvy from work surface. Set template aside.

## STEP 3: PREPARE CLOTH

Use an iron to press green linen to remove any wrinkles.

Place linen on work surface and place marked Sulky Solvy on top, positioning embroidery pattern in center.

Use painter's tape to secure Sulky Solvy to linen.

Fasten linen and attached Sulky Solvy in embroidery hoop, centering as much of embroidery pattern as possible within hoop.

## STEP 4: STITCH CARTOUCHE

Use a single strand of embroidery floss for small leaves across top of cartouche and words and letters. Use two strands of embroidery floss for all other areas.

Begin by backstitching all lines, except small berries and dashed background on face of cartouche, using floss colors of your choice.

Next, add French knots for small berries.

Last, use small running stitches to create dashed background on face of cartouche.

Gently shift embroidery hoop, if necessary, as you complete each section to start work on next.

## STEP 5: REMOVE SULKY SOLVY

When embroidery is completed, remove embroidery hoop.

Gently tear away any large pieces of Sulky Solvy and discard or save them for small projects.

Soak embroidered fabric in cool water for at least an hour to remove remaining Sulky Solvy. Be sure all starch fragments are dissolved.

Spread out fabric flat on towel to dry. When nearly dry, place embroidered fabric face down on towel and gently press with iron.

Your cartouche is now ready to embellish a handmade gift of your choice. For quilt shown on page 153, raw edges of cartouche were turned under and the embroidered cartouche was blind-stitched onto corner.

# CARTOUCHES AND THE CARTOGRAPHIC ARTS

You may have seen a cartouche in any number of places and not realized it: carved in marble over a doorway, added at the base of a painting or a print, drawn on a historical map. A cartouche is an ornate frame, usually surrounding some detail about the place or work to which it is attached.

Sometimes a cartouche looks like a sheet of paper with elaborately scrolled edges, and in fact, this type of ornament gets its name from the French word for cartridge, a gunpowder-filled rolled tube of paper. Cartouches were very popular in hieroglyphics, but the cartouche's popularity in European design of all kinds rose in the Baroque era, and the ornament came into its own on sixteenth-century engraved maps.

A map's cartouche plays both functional and decorative roles. It may contain identifying information about the region depicted on the map, or the name and coat of arms of the patron to whom the map is dedicated, or the individual engravers or cartographers responsible for the map's creation. It also provides an opportunity for elaborate decoration, and cartouches found on early maps might be bursting with plants and animals, or flanked by elaborately clothed human figures. You might see a cartouche with otters and beavers, plants native to the mapped region, or representations of the region's inhabitants.

On modern maps, ornate cartouches and other artistic map details have fallen from favor and been replaced by more purely functional elements, but the visual language of the cartouche maintains its appeal. It was after studying a number of such ornamental cartouches found on early printed maps that artist Rebecca Ringquist was inspired to create her hand-stitched version, which you can make and use to label a quilt or other handmade gift (see page 152).

Read more about cartouches and the art of mapmaking in these books:

*Art and Cartography: Six Historical Essays.* D. Woodward, ed. Chicago: University Press of Chicago, 1987.

*Baroque Cartouches for Designers and Artists: 136 Plates from the "Historische Bilder-Bibel" designed and engraved by Johann Ulrich Krauss, with an introduction by Edward A. Maser.* Johann Ulrich Krauss. New York: Dover, 1969.

*Decorative Printed Maps of the 15th to 18th Centuries; a rev. ed. of Old Decorative Maps and Charts, by A. L. Humphreys.* R. A. Skelton. London & New York: Staples Press, 1952.

*Recueil de Cartouches.* H. Vredeman de Vries. Brussels, 1870.

See more maps online here:

Osher Map Library's online exhibitions: http://usm.maine.edu/maps/exhibitions

Discovery and Exploration maps at the Library of Congress: www.loc.gov/collection/discovery-and-exploration/about-this-collection

Use these Subject Headings to find more resources on cartouches and early maps:

CARTOUCHES, ORNAMENTAL (DECORATIVE ARTS).
CARTOUCHES, ORNAMENTAL (DECORATIVE ARTS) — HISTORY.
DECORATION AND ORNAMENT, BAROQUE.
EARLY MAPS.
EARLY MAPS — FACSIMILES.
MAPS — ILLUSTRATIONS.

And if you're interested in reading more about historical maps, turn to page 162 to learn more about early hand-drawn portolan charts.

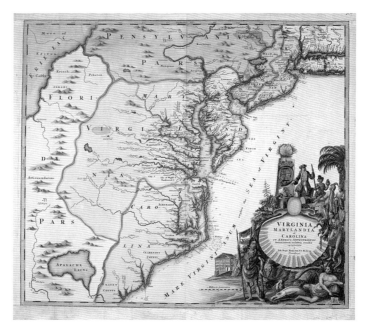

RIGHT This eighteenth-century map was meant to stimulate emigration to the North American colonies. Its cartouche is dramatically embellished with bountiful flora and fauna, human figures, and scenes of tobacco production.

# Rhumb Lines Wall Hanging

## DESIGNED BY JESSICA PIGZA

ABOVE Battista Agnese included a web of rhumb lines when he created this sixteenth-century hand-drawn map of Cyprus.

Rhumb lines were once a means for sailors using nautical maps known as portolan charts to navigate the seas. These lines, laid out in a regular geometric grid by plotting equally spaced points around a central point and then connecting those points, provided the navigational guidance a sailor needed to find his way from one port to another in the Mediterranean during the thirteenth-century.

When I studied the webs of colorful and complex rhumb lines on a number of portolan charts available for viewing via libraries' online collections, I imagined them as a stitched geometric design stretched across a wall, and the Rhumb Lines Wall Hanging is the result.

BEYOND THIS PROJECT:

By studying images of portolan charts, you could devise your own pattern with differing densities of intersecting lines. You might also consider choosing colors to reflect those traditionally used to mark rhumb lines—rich green, gold, red, and black—or adding an embroidered compass rose or other visual elements seen on portolan charts. You could simply adapt the pattern here to make something larger in scale (like a throw, stitched on thick cozy wool) or smaller (like a pillow or a dainty neckerchief).

You'll find additional resources for finding and learning about portolan charts on page 162. And if you're interested in learning more about the history of cartography and the inspirational possibilities of maps, turn to page 156 and check out fiber artist Rebecca Ringquist's project on page 152.

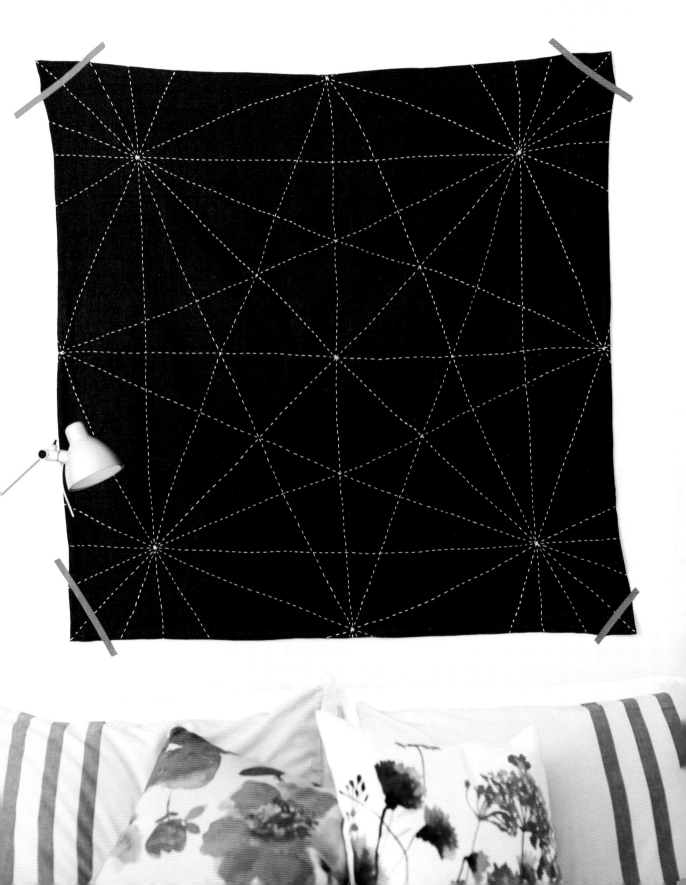

## FINISHED DIMENSIONS

- 41 × 41" (104 × 104cm) square

## SUPPLIES

- 42" (107cm) square piece of blue linen
- Iron and ironing board
- Erasable fabric-marking pen or removable tailor's chalk
- Yardstick
- 2 skeins white sashiko embroidery thread
- Embroidery needle
- Thread, in color to match linen
- Hand-sewing needle

## STEP 1: PREPARE FABRIC

Wash and dry fabric to eliminate later
shrinkage. Iron to remove wrinkles.

## STEP 2: MARK RHUMB LINES

Fold fabric twice to form a square 4
layers thick. Iron folds, then open
fabric and mark fold lines with erasable
fabric-marking pen.

Fold fabric twice again, this time
diagonally, to form a triangle 4 layers
thick. Iron folds, then open fabric and
mark these fold lines with erasable
fabric-marking pen.

When laid flat, fabric should now have
a total of 8 lines radiating out from a
central point.

Use a yardstick to measure and mark a
dot 19½" (50cm) out from central point
along each of 8 radiating lines.

Following diagram on page 161, use a
yardstick and erasable fabric-marking pen
to connect dots with lines.

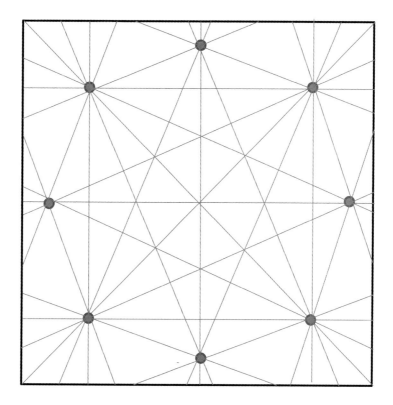

### STEP 3: STITCH RHUMB LINES

Use white sashiko thread to go over each
marked line with a running stitch. For
each line, cut a length of sashiko thread
about 8" (20cm) longer than the line you
will stitch, so entire line can be stitched
without need to knot off partway across.

Before knotting off each completed line,
gently flatten and straighten fabric along
length of line to ease stitches' tension
and prevent fabric from puckering.

Although finished work will be largely
reversible, be sure to designate one side
as wrong side and one to be right side.
Place stitches so that a stitch stretches
across places marked with dots on right
side of wall hanging, to create small star
patterns of crossing stitches. Place knots
at start and finish of each line on wrong
side of wall hanging, so that all knots can
be hidden by hem in next step.

### STEP 4: HEM WALL HANGING

Turn all 4 edges of wall hanging under ¼"
(5mm) and press fold. Turn edges under
another ¼" (5mm) and press fold. (Double-
folded hem will hide all end knots.)

Using all-purpose thread, hand-stitch
along hem all the way around wall hanging,
using small running stitches or, if
desired, blind stitches.

### STEP 5: COMPLETE WALL HANGING

Following manufacturer's instructions on
fabric-marking pen, remove any visible
lines remaining on fabric.

Iron wall hanging. Hang it as desired on
your wall.

# PORTOLAN CHARTS

Long before the emergence of engraved maps, there were one-of-a-kind hand-drawn maps that captured sailors' practical knowledge and experience. Hand-drawn maps created in thirteenth-century Venice and Genoa for sailors' use as they navigated the nearby Mediterranean Sea were known as portolan charts.

Not many portolan charts survive today. But some libraries hold examples of this type of cartographic art in their map collections, and—luckily for us—some have been scanned and are available for viewing online.

Every portolan chart is a unique work of art, hand-drawn with vivid pigments on a field of vellum. These charts were created to be practical and portable navigational tools, but they contain captivating details as well, such as place names, visual landmarks for ports, and other images evocative of the locations they depict. And covering the entirety of a portolan chart is a series of angled intersecting lines called rhumb lines, often drawn in red, green, gold, and black. These rhumb lines guided sailors from place to place. And it was these rhumb lines that guided me to the idea for a geometrically stitched wall hanging (see page 158).

Libraries that have shared images of their portolan charts online include:

The British Library: www.bl.uk/onlinegallery/index.html (In their online gallery, search for "portolan")

The Beinecke Library at Yale University: http://beinecke.library.yale.edu/digitallibrary/portolan.html

University of Minnesota's James Ford Bell Library Digital exhibition: www.lib.umn.edu/apps/bell/map/PORTO/porto.html

National Maritime Museum, Great Britain: http://collections.rmg.co.uk/collections.html#!cbrowse (search for "portolan")

Other libraries that hold portolan charts include the Huntington Library of California, the Bodleian Library of Oxford University, the Newberry Library of Chicago, and the Library of Congress in Washington, DC.

If you'd like to learn more about the history of nautical mapmaking, check out these books:

*Finding Their Way at Sea: The Story of Portolan Charts, the Cartographers Who Drew Them, and the Mariners Who Sailed by Them.* Richard L. Pflederer. Houten: Hes & De Graaf, 2012

*The History of Cartography*, volume one (*Cartography in Prehistoric, Ancient, and Medieval Europe, and the Mediterranean*). J. B. Harley and David Woodward, editors. Chicago: University of Chicago Press, 1987.

*The Sea Chart: An Historical Survey based on the Collections in the National Maritime Museum.* Derek Howse and Michael Sanderson. New York: McGraw-Hill, 1973.

*Sea Charts of the Early Explorers: 13th to 17th Century.* Michel Mollat Du Jourdin and Monique de La Ronciere. New York: Thames and Hudson, 1984.

*The Charting of the Oceans: Ten Centuries of Maritime Maps.* Peter Whitfield. Rohnert Park: Pomegranate Artbooks, 1996.

You can use these Subject Headings to find more library books on these topics, too:

EARLY MAPS.
NAUTICAL CHARTS — HISTORY.

ABOVE This 1586 portolan chart, with its many pictorial
elements, was created by Edmond Doran.

163

# Japanese Heraldry Coasters

## DESIGNED BY MOLLY SCHNICK

ABOUT THE ARTIST

Molly Schnick is a Brooklyn-based designer, artist, and musician. She designs and prints her own textiles for her independent line, Jean on Jean and she is also a full-time project designer for the popular Purl Bee blog. You'll find her online at http://jeanonjeantextiles.com and www.purlbee.com/the-purl-bee/category/mollys-sketchbook.

When textile artist Molly Schnick first encountered Japanese heraldry designs, she was immediately struck by their similarity to Hawaiian quilting motifs, with patterns radiating out from a single center point. She recognized how these designs, just as in the organic and plantlike patterns on Hawaiian quilts, could have been made by carefully folding and cutting paper, in the same way that you might create a paper snowflake. And in this elegant simplicity she saw their potential as colorful circular appliqués.

The options, she told me, were overwhelming at first; there were thousands of examples just in the volumes she paged through (including those listed on page 169). She eventually narrowed her choices to the five forms given here, which she selected for their plant- and flowerlike shapes.

BEYOND THIS PROJECT:

Japanese heraldry designs can be applied to projects of all kinds, and the templates provided here are just a few of the great variety that you'll find when studying the sources listed on page 169. A combination of pinecone and evergreen heraldry designs done in frosty greens and whites could become wintry-themed coasters, or you might find a friend's favorite flower as it appears in a Japanese heraldry design and use it to create coasters in her favorite color. You could make a larger version of the coasters to cover a cork trivet or create a large-scale fabric screen using these designs, or even a template to use in etching a set of glassware. And when cut from paper, these circular forms could be used to create cards for all seasons.

- 4" (10cm) in diameter

SUPPLIES

- Pencil and paper
- Paper scissors
- Straight pins
- 4 × 8" (10 × 20cm) piece of felt in color A, for crest and inner circle
- 4 × 8" (10 × 20cm) piece of felt in color B, for outer circles
- Fabric scissors
- ¼ yard (23cm) of iron-on adhesive, such as Heat'n Bond Lite
- Iron and ironing board
- Size 8 pearl cotton thread, in colors to match each felt color
- Hand-sewing needle, with eye large enough to accommodate pearl cotton thread

Note: Each coaster is constructed of four felt layers: two outer circles, one slightly smaller inner circle that gets stitched between the two outer circles, and an appliquéd crest layer on top. The coaster's inner circle layer will not be visible once the coaster is constructed.

### STEP 1: CUT OUT TEMPLATES
Photocopy templates for outer circle, inner circle, and crest of your choice on page 167 at 160%. Using paper scissors, cut them out.

### STEP 2: CUT OUT INNER AND OUTER FELT CIRCLES
Using inner and outer circle templates as cutting guides, cut out one inner circle from felt color A and two outer circles from felt color B.

### STEP 3: CUT OUT CREST SHAPE
Cut a 4" (10cm) square from remaining felt in color A and a 4" (10cm) square from adhesive. Following instructions on adhesive package, iron adhesive to wrong side of felt. (Do not peel off the paper backing.)

Using a pencil, trace crest template onto paper backing of adhesive on felt square.

Cut out crest shape, carefully cutting through both paper backing and felt, using pencil lines of crest pattern as your guide.

### STEP 4: APPLIQUÉ CREST SHAPE ONTO ONE OF OUTER CIRCLES
Carefully peel paper backing from crest shape. Center crest shape, adhesive side down, on one of outer circles, and pin it in place. Following instructions on adhesive package, iron crest pattern into place.

Using pearl cotton thread to match color A, stitch crest to outer circle around its edges with a very small running stitch, beginning and ending on the back so knots are not visible. (Side with crest will be top of coaster.)

### STEP 5: STITCH COASTER LAYERS TOGETHER
Stack 3 circles together in this order: outer circle with appliquéd crest facing out, inner circle, and second outer circle. Pin layers together, making sure inner circle is centered so its edges are hidden when outer circles are stitched together. Using thread to match color B, stitch outer circles together around edge with a small running stitch. (Inner circle will be completely enclosed and hidden.) To hide starting knot, begin first stitch inside felt sandwich, between layers, bringing needle to outside edge of felt circle.

When you've stitched back around to beginning, pull needle and thread through just one layer of felt and tie a knot between two layers. Then pull needle through just back layer of felt and out toward center of circle. Snip thread at exit point.

167

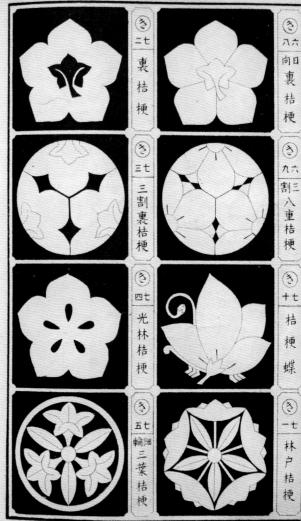

ABOVE The title of this 1915 work, *Ten Thousand Designs*,
is no exaggeration. Its delicate pages contain that many
examples of Japanese family crests.

# THE ART OF HERALDRY

Studying the history and art of heraldry is like immersing yourself in a new language—of colors, patterns, nomenclature, and symbols. In Western Europe, elaborate heraldic coats of arms were constructed from multiple elements such as a crest, shield, and family motto. These were first devised in the Middle Ages to identify participants (and their pedigrees) in courtly tournament play, or to assist in separating friend from foe on the battlefield.

Heraldic arts can be found far beyond the European courts, however. In Japan, the heraldic traditions took root in the twelfth-century out of a similar need for identification on the battlefield. The crests chosen were often based on historic designs used long before by Japanese families of nobility. These crests, called *mon* or *monsho*, usually took a circular form, made use of just two colors, and often depicted plants and animals. From rabbits to plum blossoms, tortoises to hollyhocks, herons to chrysanthemums, there are thousands of design elements and subtle variations from crest to crest.

Heraldry appears in many forms when it comes to libraries and their collections, from bindings stamped with previous owner's coats of arms to bookplates bearing family crests. Libraries with significant genealogy collections have guides to heraldry that help those studying their family history to identify their coat of arms. Heraldry guides can also help you design your own coat of arms. And once you've designed it, you can then create a bookplate, fabric stencil, or papercut letterhead design that represents you personally.

These books offer introductions to the language and history of heraldic arts in both the European and Japanese traditions:

*Heraldry for the Designer*. William Metzig. New York: Van Nostrand Reinhold, 1970.

*Heraldry: An Introduction to a Noble Tradition*. Michel Pastoureau. New York: Harry N. Abrams, 1997.

*Ten Thousand Designs, Compiled by Kotani Heishichi*. Kyoto: Honda Ichijiro, 1915.

*The Elements of Japanese Design: A Handbook of Family Crests, Heraldry & Symbolism; with over 2,700 crests drawn by Kiyoshi Kawamoto*. John W. Dower. New York and Tokyo: Weatherhill, 2000.

*Handbook of Designs and Motifs*. Introduction by P. K. Thomajan. New York: Tudor Publishing Company, 1950.

*Japanese Emblems and Designs*. Walter Amstutz. Introduction by J. Hillier. New York: Dover Publications, 1994.

Use these Subject Headings to find more resources on heraldry, especially Japanese heraldry:

Color in Heraldry.

Crests — Japan.

Devices (Heraldry).

Devices (Heraldry) — Japan.

Heraldry.

Heraldry — History.

Heraldry — Japan.

# Patchwork Pyramids

## DESIGNED BY BRETT BARA

ABOUT THE ARTIST
Brett Bara is a New York-based designer who specializes in crafts, desserts, and DIY décor. She is the author of the book *Sewing in a Straight Line*, host of the Emmy-nominated television series *Knit & Crochet Now*, and founder of Brooklyn Craft Company and Brooklyn Craft Camp. In addition to her regular contributions to the popular blog Design*Sponge, you'll also find her online at www.brooklyncraftcompany.com.

An applied mathematics textbook might not sound like the sort of thing to lead you to pick up needle and thread. Nevertheless, designer and crafter Brett Bara found creative inspiration in the pages of a 1905 textbook by Edward F. Worst called *Constructive Work: Its Relation to Number, Literature, History, and Nature Work*, and created a pattern for a trio of patchwork pyramids that can be used as soft sculptures, children's toys, and more.

For Brett, this textbook offered a great reminder that, despite the technology we live with today, some things haven't changed. Brett explained: "Crafts like sewing, knitting, and papercraft are still a great way to learn math, and the geometric shapes demonstrated in this book are a staple of design that never goes out of style."

Pyramids and triangles have a growing prominence in the design world, and when Brett came across a section in *Constructive Work* that featured triangular shapes, she knew she wanted to create patchwork pyramids that would combine the lessons in this historical text with twenty-first-century trends in the design and quilting worlds.

BEYOND THIS PROJECT:

The pyramid lends itself to easy interpretation in a variety of sizes for different purposes. One useful variation I've made is a pair of pyramids about half the size of Brett's smallest ones, with weighted bases. These pyramid weights hold a book open while you read, leaving your hands free to sketch or take notes. To make a pair of pyramid book weights, stuff their tops firmly with fiberfill, and insert something heavy inside at the base, like clean pebbles, a length of chain from the hardware store, or a small handful of ball bearings. Then, hand-stitch the opening closed. Using the same method, you could make an extra-large weighted pyramid to use as a soft doorstop.

FINISHED DIMENSIONS

- Small pyramid: 5" (13cm) tall × 3½" (9cm) wide
- Medium pyramid: 6" (15cm) tall × 3½" (9cm) wide
- Large pyramid: 7" (18cm) tall × 5" (13cm) wide

SUPPLIES

- ½ yard (46cm) medium-weight nonwoven fusible interfacing
- Ruler
- Pencil
- Fabric scissors
- ¼ yard (46cm) each of 5 quilting-weight fabrics, in coordinating colors
- Straight pins
- Sewing machine
- Thread, in a color to match your fabric
- Iron and ironing board
- Fiberfill
- Pointy object, such as a chopstick or knitting needle
- Hand-sewing needle

Note: The instructions for sewing all three pyramids are the same. Just use the appropriate measurements for each pyramid according to Figures A and B, which list size small measurements first, followed by sizes medium and large in parentheses. There is enough fabric for one small, one medium, and one large pyramid.

STEP 1: MEASURE AND CUT INTERFACING

Fold interfacing in half. Following dimensions in Figure A, use a ruler and pencil to measure along fold line, marking two points for pyramid height. Then, measure as indicated in Figure A, and mark two points for base. (For example, to make a small pyramid, measure 5½" (14cm) along fold line and 2" (5cm) from fold line along bottom edge.) Draw a line to connect base line to height line, forming a triangle.

Cut out triangle shape through both layers of interfacing and unfold. This will be one side of pyramid. Use this triangle as guide to cut 3 more matching triangles of interfacing.

Cut 1 pyramid base from interfacing according to the measurements in Figure B.

STEP 2: FUSE FABRIC AND INTERFACING AND CUT OUT SHAPES

Following instructions on interfacing package, fuse each piece of interfacing to wrong side of a different piece of fabric. Trim fabric to same dimensions as interfacing.

STEP 3: MARK CORNER POINTS

On wrong side of each piece (interfacing side), measure ¼" (5mm) from each raw edge and draw a light line around edge of piece with pencil. Mark a dot at corners where lines intersect (see Figure C).

STEP 4: SEW PYRAMID SIDES

Note: To achieve sharp corners, sew all seams between marked corner dots only. As you work, be careful not to catch any neighboring seam allowances in seam you're sewing.

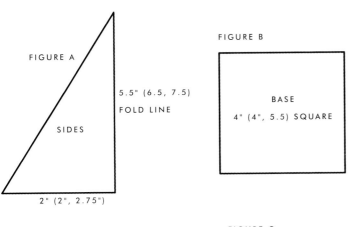

FIGURE A

5.5" (6.5, 7.5)
FOLD LINE

SIDES

2" (2", 2.75")

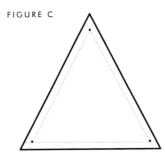

FIGURE B

BASE
4" (4", 5.5) SQUARE

FIGURE C

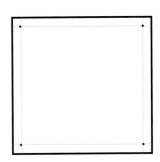

Place two pyramid sides together with right sides facing, aligning bottoms and side edges. Pin one long edge. Using a sewing machine and thread to match fabric, and leaving a ¼" (5mm) seam allowance, sew along one long edge *only between two dots*, backstitching at beginning and end of each seam to reinforce them. (Alternatively, hand-stitch seams.)

Open the two pieces and place a third pyramid side, right sides facing, along a long edge of piece you just sewed. Fold seam allowance of first two pieces so it is out of the way. Sew third piece in place, again stitching only between dots. Repeat to attach fourth piece. Press all seams to one side.

Fold entire piece with right sides facing, so two remaining raw long-side edges meet. Sew this seam as you did previous seams, but leave a 3" opening in center of seam. Press this seam, folding unsewn fabric at opening to wrong side and pressing.

## STEP 5: ATTACH PYRAMID BASE

Sew base to pyramid one side at a time, sewing a unique seam for each side of base. Do not attempt to sew around all four base sides with one continuous seam or corners will be wonky.

Place one edge of base piece along one open edge of any side piece, right sides together. Align raw edges and corners, and pin pieces together. Sew edge using a ¼" (5mm) seam allowance, *stitching only between dots*, and folding seam allowance of any neighboring seams out of way so they do not get caught in seam you're sewing. Repeat for remaining three sides of base.

## STEP 6: TURN, STUFF, AND FINISH PYRAMID

Trim seam allowances from all corners. Gently turn piece right side out, working fabric through opening in side seam. Use a pointy object to poke out corners, and press all seams. Firmly stuff pyramid with fiberfill. Whipstitch opening closed using hand-sewing needle and thread.

ABOVE *Industrial Art Text-Books*, *Constructive Work*, and *School Needlework* are just few of many early school texts that can inspire modern design by revealing arts and handicrafts education history.

# CHILDREN'S EDUCATIONAL MANUALS

Thanks to a national Arts and Crafts revival and a new educational philosophy viewing hands-on activities as central to the learning process, America's public school students in the early twentieth century learned much more than reading and writing. Although art education had been part of the public school curriculum since the 1870s, new courses were developed to include training in practical arts, handicrafts, and other manual arts—skills that, some educators argued, would be lost entirely if not offered in schools because they were no longer taught at home.

For students, this meant classes in woodworking, sewing, home economics, metalwork, and industrial drawing. And for curious craft-oriented researchers today, this means a legacy of textbooks from this period. Libraries that collect books on the history of education often have textbooks and class manuals from this period in their collections. These books can provide a glimpse into how children one hundred years ago learned to count, measure, cut, stitch, draft, draw, and weave. These little volumes also offer surprising inspiration: ideas for small useful projects, forgotten construction methods, tips for proper mending, and now-unusual material uses.

Here are just a few textbooks I've found to be informative and interesting, including *Constructive Work*, the volume that led designer Brett Bara to create her geometry lesson–inspired patchwork pyramids:

*Constructive Work: Its Relation to Number, Literature, History, and Nature Work.* Revised and enlarged ed. Edward F. Worst. Chicago: A. W. Mumford and Company, 1905.

*Industrial Art Text-Books: A Graded Course in Art in its Relation to Industry.* Bonnie E. Snow and Hugo B. Froehlich. New York: The Prang Educational Company. Various eds: 1915, 1919, 1922–1925.

*Text Books of Art Education.* Hugo B. Froehlich and Bonnie E. Snow. New York: The Prang Educational Company, 1905.

*School Needlework: A Course of Study in Sewing Designed for Use in Schools.* Olive C. Hapgood. Boston: Ginn and Company, 1892.

*Hand Sewing Lessons: A Graded Course for Schools and for the Home.* Sarah Ewell Krolik. Educational Publishing Company, 1905.

*School Arts Magazine.* Worcester, MA.: Davis, 1901.

Use these Subject Headings to find more resources on this topic:

ART — STUDY AND TEACHING.

ART — STUDY AND TEACHING — PERIODICALS.

MANUAL TRAINING — METHODS AND MANUALS.

Additionally, you will find school textbooks catalogued under the Subject Headings upon which they focus, such as:

GARMENT CUTTING.

SEWING.

NEEDLEWORK.

# Paper Towns

## DESIGNED BY SARAH GOLDSCHADT

ABOUT THE ARTIST
Sarah Goldschadt is
a Danish American
graphic designer and
crafter currently living in
Brooklyn. She is author
of *Craft-A-Day* and
coauthor of *Pom-Poms!*.
She has designed for
dozens of magazines,
including *Food Network
Magazine*, *Do It Yourself*,
*Martha Stewart Living*,
and *Architectural Digest*.
You can find her online at
http://sah-rah.com.

Artist and crafter Sarah Goldschadt first started thinking about creating a paper town after seeing a "Paperville" project in the June 1907 issue of *St. Nicholas*, a popular and influential children's magazine of the late-nineteenth and early-twentieth centuries. As she started contemplating her own project, her mind immediately leapt to the architecture that surrounded her during childhood summers spent in Copenhagen. Sarah's paper homes and apartment buildings were inspired by her memories and photographs of Danish streetscapes, and they evoke the presentation of architectural elevations in design books.

Sarah's miniature houses can be made in whatever colors you want, and the basic structures can be used to make a garland that makes a sweet housewarming gift for a friend. Or, make as many houses, apartments, and trees as you wish in a variety of colors, to create your own miniature paper town.

BEYOND THIS PROJECT:

You might use the house or apartment building on a card you send out to share your change of address or to invite friends to a housewarming party. And each building, standing on its little foot on a plate, can serve as a place card at a dinner party.

If you'd like to take inspiration from your surroundings, create a favorite street from your childhood; or, help your own kids build a paper model of the neighborhood where you live.

If you want to dig into the past to give your paper town some historical touches, early books on architecture can offer up a variety of illustrations of castles, villas, ancient churches, and other historical structures. Turn to page 182 to learn more about finding architectural books and books about the built world of your favorite places.

- House: 1⅞" (4.8cm) tall by 1½" (4cm) wide
- Apartment: 2¼" (5.7cm) tall by 1½" (4cm) wide
- Tree: 1½" (4cm) tall by 1" (2.5cm) wide

SUPPLIES

- Cardstock in a variety of colors
- Paper scissors
- Pencil
- Fine-tip permanent markers in colors of your choice
- Craft glue
- Scotch tape (optional)
- Cutting mat (optional)
- Pushpin (optional)
- Tapestry needle (optional)
- Baker's twine (optional)

### STEP 1: CREATE TEMPLATES

Photocopy templates on page 181 for house, apartment building, building "feet," and pine trees at 125%. Cut them out.

### STEP 2: CREATE BUILDINGS

Use a pencil to trace house and apartment building templates onto card stock, varying colors as you desire. Cut out as many of each main building shape as desired.

If you would like your buildings to have different-colored paper elements: Using the template as a guide, cut out large details, such as a roof section or door, from different colors of cardstock and glue them over building base.

Using template as a guide to placement, draw in window and door details, using a fine-tip permanent marker. Include as many details as you wish such as roof tiles or curtains.

### STEP 3: CREATE PINE TREES

Trace tree templates onto green cardstock. Cut out, including center slits, and slide the two halves together.

### TO MAKE HOUSES AND APARTMENT BUILDINGS INTO A PAPER TOWN:

For each house or apartment building, cut a "foot" from matching cardstock.

Fold foot in half, short ends together. Glue or tape one half in the center of the back of the house or building, with other half extending out from bottom of house. This long free foot, when bent back behind house, allows house to stand up. Arrange a variety of stand-alone houses and buildings on a large sheet of cardstock and glue or tape down their feet to create a paper town.

### TO MAKE GARLANDS:

Place a finished house or apartment building face up on a cutting mat. Use a pushpin to pierce two holes in it, just at roofline, about ⅛" (3mm) in from right and left sides. Repeat with as many houses or apartment buildings as you wish to use on garland.

Use a tapestry needle and baker's twine to string buildings together. Insert needle through hole on front side and then bring it up through next pinhole from wrong side; move to next house and insert needle from front side again. This will keep twine hidden behind houses. Leave a long enough tail of twine at each end of garland for hanging where you wish.

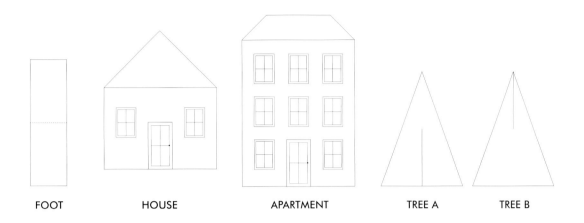

FOOT          HOUSE          APARTMENT          TREE A          TREE B

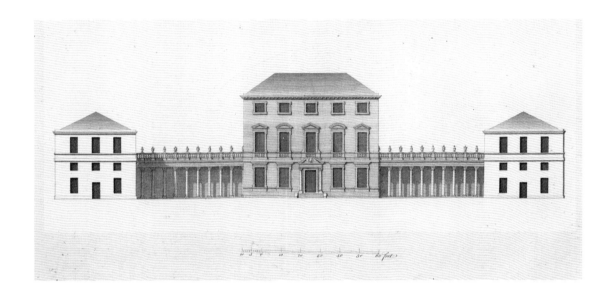

Architectural elevations can be technical, like this 1756 engraving, or more whimsical, like Sarah's paper houses.

# ARCHITECTURE AROUND THE WORLD

Whether you document your own travels—with photographs and sketches of landscapes, buildings, or people—or you visit faraway places vicariously through illustrated guidebooks, the worlds of travel and architecture offer unending inspiration.

If you're curious about how things are made, built, and grown all around the world, you might start with historical travel guides. Local libraries may have only the most recent editions of a guidebook, but by checking the holdings of research libraries you can uncover older editions that offer glimpses of places, people, and local traditions from times past. To find guidebooks in a library catalog, identify a place's Subject Heading and then add a "Guidebooks" subdivision to refine the search. For example, to find out more about Copenhagen, which was one of artist Sarah Goldschadt's inspirations when designing her paper towns project (see page 176), you could search for:

> COPENHAGEN (DENMARK) — GUIDEBOOKS.
> COPENHAGEN (DENMARK) — BUILDINGS, STRUCTURES, ETC. — GUIDEBOOKS.
> SCANDINAVIA — GUIDEBOOKS.

Architectural elevations offer particular visual appeal when searching for examples of what the built world looks like. These depict the front view or facade of a building, and they are ideal candidates for being repurposed for paper towns like Sarah's or for collage art, linear embroideries, or other architecture-themed design projects. You can find architectural elevations by searching for books with these Subject Headings, and then finding titles that mention they include elevations:

> ARCHITECTURE — DESIGNS AND PLANS.
> ARCHITECTURE, DOMESTIC — DESIGNS AND PLANS.

If it's the architecture of the everyday that interests you, searching under the Subject Heading "Vernacular Architecture" will get you started. Here are two books that are good starting points for the topic:

*Encyclopedia of Vernacular Architecture*. Paul Oliver. Cambridge, UK; New York: Cambridge University Press, 1997.

*Atlas of Vernacular Architecture of the World*. Marcel Vellinga, Paul Oliver, and Alexander Bridge. Abingdon, Oxon; New York: Routledge, 2007.

Whatever historical or geographical direction your research takes, I hope that the journey yields interesting images, insights, and design ideas for the future.

Fig. 5. Be careful to paste them down to the *very lower edge* of the house. Do *not* by any chance paste them as shown in Fig. 6, for you may see at a glance that here there is nothing to prevent the house from falling backward and the feet closing up like a hinge. If pasted as in Fig. 5 the house will be practically as firm as if it were made with four sides.

It is better to have the objects slant *back* a little. If they slant too far backward or forward, trim the bottom edge of the feet to correct this. Sometimes the bottom edges of the houses will have to come off a trifle, but this is a simple matter, and will be per-

simple and easy-to-make objects can be made very effective when properly grouped.

FIG. 8.  A SCENE IN PAPERVILLE.

FIG. 9.  ANOTHER SCENE IN PAPERVILLE.

fectly clear as soon as you actually come to set them up on the floor or large table.

It may not be clear how a tall flagstaff made of thin paper can be made to stand. This, too is very simple. Take a strip about ½ inch wide and fold it in half along its length, then open it out so that the two sides will form a right angle, when the staff will be found to be quite rigid. A tall tree if top-heavy may be strengthened by pasting such an "angle iron" along the trunk and up into the tops.

The houses and other objects shown in the illustrations were purposely constructed in "home-made" style in order to show that very

A variation of the "game" may be had by constructing houses, etc., of varying sizes—though all smaller than the first ones made—and then setting these up in the background, the smallest ones the furthest off, and the largest ones in the nearest foreground. This will cleverly give the idea of perspective and distance, and the effect will be quite realistic. Of course this is suggested only for the larger children who have exhausted their interest in the simpler street-front arrangement of the houses.

A hill or rolling country may be imitated by throwing a piece of green or brown cloth over a pile of loosely crumpled tissue

FIG. 10.  ONE OF THE FASHIONABLE STREETS OF PAPERVILLE.

or other paper. The hill shown in Fig. 11 was nothing more than a child's brown linen apron resting on such a pile of loose newspaper.

# Cuts of Meat Table Runner

## DESIGNED BY JESSICA PIGZA

Early cookbooks didn't contain the wealth of visual material we've come to expect in cookbooks today, but certain categories of artwork did find their way into these books as a means of providing guidance to the reader. For example, some historical cookbooks include foldout engravings showing the proper way to arrange serving dishes or how to decorate a table to best effect.

In looking at older diagrams of various cuts of meat in a number of late-nineteenth and early-twentieth-century editions of *Mrs. Owens' New Cook Book and Complete Household Manual*, I was intrigued by their shapes and began to picture them in hand-stitching. This project, with three designs to be embroidered on a linen table runner, is the result of the sketches that I made while studying the cow, pig, and sheep diagrams in this little volume.

When making this project, you have the option to use all three images or just those that strike your fancy.

BEYOND THIS PROJECT:

These designs can be adapted and used for any number of embroidery projects that would make perfect gifts for a friend who embraces nose-to-tail eating, from embellishing an apron front to adding small-scale versions to the corner of cloth napkins to enlarging each animal design to adorn a placemat.

If you'd like hints on finding more historical cookbooks and cookbook art, see page 188.

- 11 × 72" (28 × 183cm)

SUPPLIES

- Two 12 × 73" (30 × 185cm) pieces pale beige linen or linen-cotton blend
- Iron and ironing board
- Double-sided tape
- Erasable fabric-marking pen
- Embroidery hoop
- 2 skeins each of sashiko embroidery thread in blue and red
- Embroidery needle
- Sewing machine
- Fabric scissors
- Thread, in color to match linen
- Pins

### STEP 1: PREPARE FABRIC

Wash and dry fabric to eliminate later shrinkage.

Iron fabric to remove any wrinkles.

### STEP 2: PREPARE TEMPLATE

Photocopy and enlarge templates of your choice on page 187 by 200%. If you wish to reverse the direction of any animal template, copy it and use a light box and a permanent marker to trace pattern onto reverse side of paper.

### STEP 3: TRANSFER STITCHING PATTERN TO LINEN

Place one of linen pieces on a smooth surface, right side down. Carefully place each photocopied design, right side down, on fabric, positioning each animal where you want that embroidery design to appear. Attach outer edges of paper to fabric using double-sided tape and press gently to secure.

Flip layers so fabric is facing up and photocopied patterns are attached beneath it, and place them over a bright light source, such as a light box. Trace design from pattern onto linen using an erasable fabric-marking pen. (If you don't have a

light box, you can hold layers up against a sunny window instead. Use masking tape to hold fabric and paper flat against window while you trace.)

Gently peel off pattern and double-sided tape from fabric's wrong side.

### STEP 4: STITCH DESIGN

Place fabric in an embroidery hoop.

Using blue sashiko thread and an embroidery needle, backstitch all solid lines on the design and use a running stitch for all dotted lines.

When embroidery is completed, remove linen from embroidery hoop. Following manufacturer's instructions, remove any visible traces of erasable fabric-marking pen.

Place embroidered linen facedown on a fluffy towel. Gently press with an iron.

### STEP 5: CONSTRUCT TABLE RUNNER

With right sides together, pin all around edges of two pieces of linen. Use sewing machine and all-purpose thread that matches linen to sew all around table runner's edge, using a ½" (1.2cm) seam allowance and leaving an 8" (20cm) opening at center of bottom seam.

Clip the four corners of the two sewn layers diagonally, cutting close to corner seam but not cutting through it. This will allow corners to easily turn right side out.

Turn table runner right side out through bottom opening, making sure to fully turn out corners.

Use a hand-sewing needle and all-purpose thread to whipstitch opening closed.

Place finished table runner facedown on a fluffy towel and gently press it with an iron.

### STEP 6: ADD TOP STITCHING

Using red sashiko thread and an embroidery needle, place a line of running stitches ½" (1.2cm) from edge of table runner around all four sides.

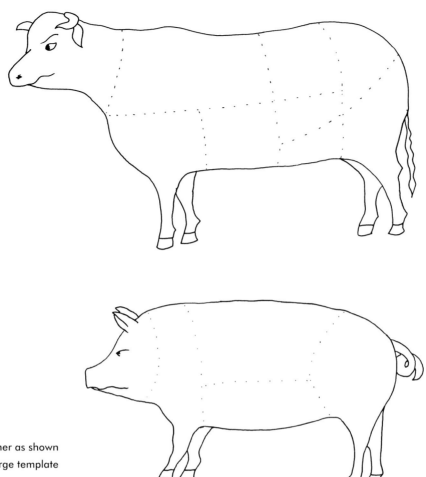

To make table runner as shown
on page 185, enlarge template
by 200%.

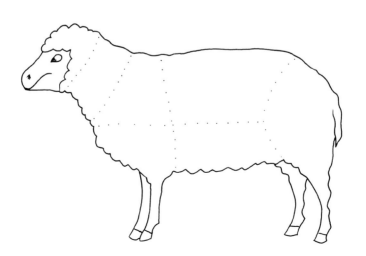

# CULINARY ARTS

When it comes to early printed books in libraries, one of the most accessible and fascinating topics is food. From very early housekeeping guides to "receipt" books full of early recipes for food as well as home remedies for humans and animals alike, these texts offer a mix of the familiar and the strange. Even if you aren't a scholar with a deep knowledge of the topic, you can often relate immediately to at least some portions of an early printed cookbook.

In a single volume from the seventeenth-or eighteenth-century, you might read about how to preserve and cook foods, bake breads and cakes, and make wine or beer. You might also learn about caring for livestock, mixing healing remedies, and managing servants. And while the recipes themselves bear little resemblance to the exacting ingredient lists, step-by-step instructions, and comforting details written into recipes today, you'll find plenty of familiar dishes and still-common approaches to cooking.

Use these sources to learn more about culinary history:

*A History of Food.* Maguelonne Toussaint-Samat; translated by Anthea Bell. Chichester, West Sussex, U.K.; Malden, MA: Wiley-Blackwell, 2009.

*Cambridge World History of Food.* Kenneth F. Kiple and Kriemhild Coneè Ornelas. Cambridge, UK; New York: Cambridge University Press, 2000.

*Printed Cookbooks in Europe, 1470–1700: A Bibliography of Early Modern Culinary Literature.* Henry Notaker. New Castle, DE: Oak Knoll Press; Houten, Netherlands; Hes & De Graf Publishers, 2010.

Lowenstein, Eleanor. *Bibliography of American Cookery Books, 1742–1860. Based on Waldo Lincoln's American Cookery Books, 1742–1860.* Worcester, MA: American Antiquarian Society, 1972.

Food Timeline (created and maintained by Lynne Olver, a food historian with a masters degree in library science): www.foodtimeline.org

Feeding America: The Historic American Cookbook Project (from Michigan State University Libraries): http://digital.lib.msu.edu/projects cookbooks

When searching in a library catalog, try keywords like "cookery" and "receipts" because they will often lead to older historical materials, and try the following Subject Headings:

Cookbooks.
Cookbooks — Europe — History
— Early Works to 1800 —
Bibliography.
Cooking.
Cooking, American — Bibliography.
Food — History.
Food Habits — History.
Meat Cuts.

# FARMERS' DEPARTMENT.

### CUTTING UP MEATS. DISEASES OF ANIMALS.
### ROAD-MAKING. MISCELLANEOUS.

## CUTTING UP MEATS.

 E give diagrams showing the manner of cutting up meats at the present day for home consumption. Packers have a different method. On the quarter of beef the figures are made to correspond with the like parts in the beef on foot. It is the same with the porker.

### BEEF.

1. Cheek, for soup.
2. Neck, for mince-meat.
3. Chuck, for roasting.
4. Rib roast—best roast.
5. Porter-house steak.
6. Sirloin, roast or steak.
7. Rump, to roast or boil.
8. Round, for steak, pot-roast, or dried beef.
9. Hock, for soup-meat.
10. Shank, for soup-bone.
11. Flank, for soup or steak.
12. Rib or plate, for corned beef.
13. Brisket, for corned beef.
14. Shoulder-clod, for pot-roast.
15. Shank, for soup-bone.
16. Breast, for soup or stew.

The pluck is the heart, liver, and lights.

RIGHT This 1892 edition of *Mrs. Owens' New Cook Book,* like many historical cookbooks, includes much more than just recipes.

# Radish Love Tote

## DESIGNED BY JESSICA PIGZA

**The hearts and leaves on this early twentieth-century design by Henri Gillet were on my mind as I sketched my radish form.**

I started playing around with vegetable silhouettes one day after reading an article about Victory Gardens and learning a bit about World War II's propaganda campaigns. The artists who created posters promoting gardening on the home front really made their vegetables look like heroes, and I wanted my design to be just as bold. The heart-shaped ruby radish stencil is the result: a can-do visual reminder to myself to visit my local farmer's market more often and eat more vegetables each and every day.

You can add this stencil to a prepurchased plain tote. Or, if you're like me and experience no shortage of promotional tote bags in your life, you can add the design to the blank side of one of those freebies instead, and create a mixed message of propaganda of your very own.

BEYOND THIS PROJECT:

A stencil is, by its nature, adaptable to all kinds of surface decoration projects. The radishes in this project's repeating pattern can become the border of a tablecloth, for instance, or could be added to an apron. If you'd like to explore other veggie graphic possibilities, take a look at the variety of Victory Garden posters (see page 195 for tips on where to find them) and design a stencil of your own favorite veggie or fruit. You could also use it as a template for a needle-turned appliqué design on a quilt. In addition to its use on textiles, the stencil design can be adapted at a small scale as a template for cut and layered paper cards for garden-themed stationery.

FINISHED DIMENSIONS

- 15 × 15" (38 × 38cm)

SUPPLIES

- 1 white or natural cotton tote bag measuring around 15 × 15" (38 × 38cm)
- Iron and ironing board
- Two 8½ × 11" (22 × 28cm) sheets clear acetate film
- Fine-tip permanent marker
- Cutting mat
- Craft knife
- Scrap butcher paper or kraft paper
- Painter's tape
- Spoon
- Fabric paint in magenta and green*
- Small plate or dish
- Stencil brush (a small, round, stiff brush)

*Be sure the paint you buy is appropriate for fabric use, and read the instructions on proper cleanup, how to fix paint permanently, and how to care for the finished work.

### STEP 1: PREPARE TOTE
Wash tote. Use an iron to press both sides of tote flat.

### STEP 2: CREATE STENCILS
Photocopy radish template on page 193 at 100%. Center enlarged template under sheet of clear acetate. Use fine-tip permanent marker to trace design onto surface of acetate.

Place acetate on cutting mat, and use craft knife to cut out radish shape along lines you drew.

Repeat with radish greens template and second acetate sheet to create a second stencil.

### STEP 3: PREPARE TO START STENCILING
Note: This tote bag design incorporates a total of six stencil applications: three radish shapes and three radish greens shapes. You add each shape one at a time, leaving a few minutes' time for the paint to dry after completing each shape before moving on to the next one.

Cover work surface with a large sheet of butcher paper or kraft paper to protect it from paint.

Place tote bag flat on paper-covered work surface. Tuck folded piece of butcher paper or kraft paper inside tote so it lays flat. (This paper layer will prevent any paint from soaking through from one side of tote bag to other.)

### STEP 4. STENCIL RADISHES
Using project photograph on page 191 as a guide, position radish stencil in lower half of center of tote. Use painter's tape to secure stencil to tote so it won't shift while you work.

Use a spoon to add a small puddle of magenta paint to plate. Tap stencil brush up and down a few times in paint, and then apply paint to fabric within stencil area. Tapping stencil brush vigorously up and down onto fabric (instead of brushing it back and forth along surface as if you were painting a wall) will result in greater paint saturation and more vivid colors. Working in layers also helps: Cover entire stencil area with a thin layer of paint, go over it again and add a second layer, and perhaps a third layer, until you are happy with color. (No need to wait for each layer of paint to dry before adding next one.)

After you've finished stenciling this first radish shape completely, allow it to dry for a few minutes. Carefully peel back painter's tape and lift stencil off tote, being careful not to transfer any stray damp paint from stencil onto tote as you move it.

Repeat stenciling process to add one radish to left and one to right of first radish. You now have three stenciled radishes.

Allow paint to dry for an hour or so before starting on radish greens stenciling. While waiting, wash and dry dish, spoon, brush, and radish stencil, removing all traces of magenta paint. (Use cleaning method appropriate for the paint you've purchased.)

### STEP 5: STENCIL RADISH GREENS

Following same method as described in Step 4 but using green paint, stencil radish greens above each radish, lining point of radish green stem directly above heart dimple on radish top.

Allow paint to dry.

### STEP 6: SET DESIGN PERMANENTLY ON TOTE

Follow manufacturer's instructions for your paint to "set" or "fix" permanently on fabric. This may include applying heat with an iron or dryer.

Be sure to note any care instructions that accompany paint you used, so you can appropriately care for tote in future.

# YOUR VICTORY GARDEN
## counts more than ever!

WAR FOOD ADMINISTRATION

ABOVE Hubert Morley's 1945 poster was one of many
Victory Garden-themed wartime propaganda posters
to depict heroic homegrown produce.

# VICTORY GARDENS

From circus broadsides and theater announcements to travel promotions and government propaganda, posters have a long history in the United States. While posters were meant to have limited lives—displayed only until their messages no longer applied, then discarded or covered over with newer messages—all kinds of posters and broadsides have been carefully preserved in library collections. One example of bold poster design are posters printed during World War II by the Government Printing Office.

The U.S. Office of War Information worked with close to a thousand artists—some professionals, others amateurs—in the creation of poster campaigns promoting wartime economies in the early 1940s, a time when resources were severely limited. Americans encountered these posters at school or work, in libraries, and while shopping. One such campaign was the promotion of gardening on the home front, in the form of growing Victory Gardens. More than fifty million Victory Gardens were planted, and neighbors gathered together to share pressure cookers and other supplies at community canning efforts.

Looking back now, the Victory Garden campaign is viewed as having been more important for the part it played in Americans' sense of participation in the war effort than for any substantial food conservation. But that campaign, as well as other poster propaganda efforts, left behind a significant legacy of graphic design that can continue to inspire today. It was one such poster that set me on the path to create my Radish Love Tote on page 190.

You can find a variety of government-issued World War II–era posters promoting Victory Gardens and other government initiatives in libraries and government archives. And these posters, like other materials printed by the U.S. Government Printing Office, are in the public domain and are free to use in your projects.

These resources will lead to images and information on World War II–era posters:

Northwestern University Library World War II Poster Collection: http://digital.library. northwestern.edu/wwii-posters

Produce for Victory: Posters on the American Home Front (1941–45). Smithsonian Institution: http://americanhistory.si.edu/victory

*Powers of Persuasion: Poster Art from World War II*. Stacy Bredhoff. Washington, DC: National Archives, 1994. A portion of the posters included in this volume can also be viewed on the National Archives website, www.archives.gov/exhibits/ powers_of_persuasion/powers_of_persuasion_ intro.html.

Additionally, you can use these Subject Headings to find more books about posters:

War Posters.

Political Posters.

Posters.

PART THREE

APPENDIX

# STITCH GUIDE

The illustrations here show how to form the stitches used in the projects in this book. If you need more instruction, I recommend *Martha Stewart's Encyclopedia of Sewing and Fabric Crafts*, one of my favorite embroidery primers. You can also find basic instructions online if you search by stitch name.

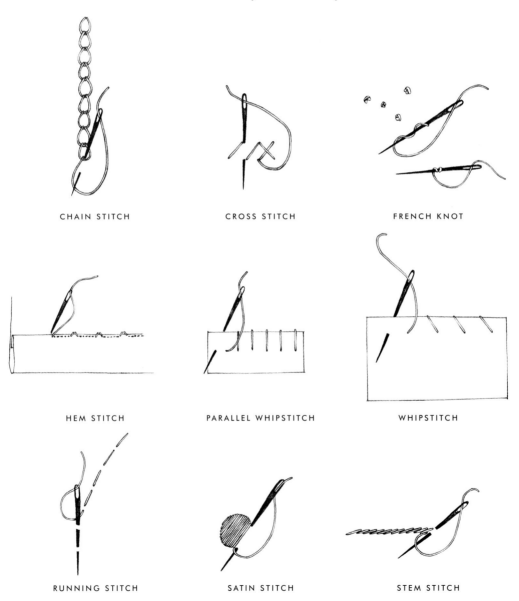

CHAIN STITCH

CROSS STITCH

FRENCH KNOT

HEM STITCH

PARALLEL WHIPSTITCH

WHIPSTITCH

RUNNING STITCH

SATIN STITCH

STEM STITCH

# SOURCES FOR SUPPLIES

Most of the fabrics, papers, notions, and tools needed to make the projects in this book can be found in your local arts and crafts and fabric shops. Below are some online sources if you can't find what you need locally.

## ARTS AND CRAFTS

A. I. FRIEDMAN
*www.aifriedman.com*

ARTIST AND CRAFTSMAN SUPPLY
*www.artistcraftsman.com*

CREATEFORLESS
*www.createforless.com*

PAPER SOURCE
*www.paper-source.com*

PEARL FINE ART SUPPLIES
*www.pearlpaint.com*

## FABRIC, EMBROIDERY, AND NOTIONS

HEDGEHOG HANDWORKS
*www.hedgehoghandworks.com*

M&J TRIMMING
*www.mjtrim.com*

PURL SOHO
*www.purlsoho.com*

STUDIO AIKA SASHIKO MATERIALS
*www.sashikodesigns.com*

## ADDITIONAL SOURCES FOR SPECIFIC PROJECTS

MARBLED FABRIC POUCH ON PAGE 62
*Iron-on vinyl and printable fabric sheets*
*CreateForLess*
*www.createforless.com*

CYANOTYPE THROW ON PAGE 118
*Coats & Clark Dual Duty Button & Craft Thread*
*Alabama Chanin*
*http://alabamachanin.com/fabric-sewing*

QUILLED WILLOW PENDANT ON PAGE 90
*Quilling papers and tools*
*J. J. Quilling Design*
*www.jjquilling.co.uk*

*WhimsiQuills*
*www.whimsiquills.com*

CARTOUCHE EMBROIDERY ON PAGE 152
*Sulky Solvy Stabilizer*
*CreateForLess*
*www.createforless.com*

FELT DOGWOOD BLOSSOMS ON PAGE 146
*White and ivory felt*
*OhMa Felt*
*http://ohmafelt.com/*

*Pom-pom fringe (pom-poms used for flower centers)*
*M&J Trimming*
*www.mjtrim.com/pompom-fringe.html*

SOIL PROFILE GROWTH CHART ON PAGE 132
*Fusible webbing*
*Mistyfuse*
*www.mistyfuse.com*

# ACKNOWLEDGMENTS

*BiblioCraft* could not have happened without the help of so many wonderful people I have had the good fortune to work with over the last seven years.

I will always be thankful to have arrived at the New York Public Library at a moment when a new culture of outreach and experimentation was on the rise, championed by Paul Leclerc, Josh Greenberg, and David Ferriero. The opportunities it created, including the chance to work with Amy Azzarito, James Murdock, and Grace Bonney on Design by the Book, were immense. I'm also grateful that both Elaine Charnov and Philip Yockey believed in my scheme to teach about vintage crafts at a research library.

My tenure at NYPL has been enriched immeasurably through the mentorship of many amazing women; my thanks especially to Ann Thornton, Vicki Steele, Denise Hibay, Kristin McDonough, and Ruth Carr for their professional care and feeding of me.

My unending thanks go to my Rare Book Division colleagues as well. Michael Inman, Ted Teodoro, and Kyle Triplett all offered good company, patience, and encouragement as this project unfolded. My thanks as well to Marguerite Nealon and Brooke Watkins for all they do in support of rare book reader services week in and week out.

I'm grateful for Rebecca Federman's enthusiasm, distraction, and supportive words. And my thanks as well to Angela Montefinise, the master of no-nonsense camaraderie, who arranged for three days of perfect lighting for photography at the library. I'm so grateful to have Annmarie Starita, Jason Bauman, and Karen Gisonny as colleagues and friends also; thank you all for keeping me grounded and fully stocked with tea and snacks.

I couldn't have completed this book if the Art and Architecture Collection staff, especially Clayton Kirking, Ryan Haley, Vincenzo Rutigliano, and Miguel Rosales had not encouraged me to wander through their stacks and to indulge my book-hoarding nature. I'm also grateful to every single member of the General Research Division for keeping up with the sheer volume of my books as they came and went. Thanks as well to Thomas Lannon and Tal Nadan for sharing their ornamental penmanship, to Matt Knutzen for sharing his map expertise, to David Christie for answering all my Anna Atkins questions, to Greg Cram for legal wisdom and good sense, and to Tom Lisanti for his illustrations advice.

My thanks to all the people who together make Handmade Crafternoons into a community of interest rather than just a series of free events: volunteers Pam Madden, Leigh Hurwitz, and Lindsy Serrano; my cohost, Maura Madden; and all my friendly attendees, including stalwarts Acacia Thompson and Mary Alice Lee. And nothing could have happened without the help of Norman Scott and his team for tables and chairs; Harry Roopnarine and his colleagues for unlocking doors and chatting with early arrivers; Brian Hurley for laptops and lights; Abby Tannenbaum for calendar listings; and Paul Delaverdac, Marie d'Origny, Jean Strouse, and Katie Pyott for sharing space.

My thanks to each and every librarian and bibliophile around the country who sent ideas and suggestions (there are too many of these helpful people to name here!). My book is far better for their recommendations. My thanks also go to the wonderful and talented designers who contributed projects to *BiblioCraft*. They are my heroes and I'm grateful to have received projects from them as well as friendship, design inspiration, support, and wise counsel.

Speaking of heroes, I'm so lucky to have had such a team at STC. My thanks to my editor, Melanie Falick, whose vision all along for my book was bigger and better than I could have imagined. I also know this book would've gone nowhere fast without the attentions of Cristina Garces, Traci Niese, and Ivy McFadden. And I remain in awe of designer Deb Wood, stylist Shana Faust, and photographer Johnny Miller and his assistant Justin Conly, whose immense talents have made *BiblioCraft* beautiful.

I'm grateful to Pearl Chin, Phyllis Howe, and everyone at Knitty City for keeping me in wool. And my thanks to the Purl Soho staff for helping me to find what I need on each and every trip (and there are many trips); I'm especially grateful to Joelle Hoverson for assisting me in a pinch with her unerring sense of color.

My thanks to my agent, Kate McKean, who makes all things happen. I'm grateful to my friends Paul Harrington, Jason Kincade, Bob Levine, Michele Whitney, and Burke Gerstenschlager for making sure I ate dinner on weekends. Jenny Bergman taught me to quilt, which was a crazy-wonderful thing to have done.

I couldn't be luckier when it comes to my entire family, and I'm grateful for their encouragement, quiet pride in my achievements, and love. And I'm so thankful to Sean Concannon, who is kind enough to believe I'm capable of doing anything I set my mind to do, even though I'm not so sure. Finally, *BiblioCraft* is dedicated to the memory of my grandmother Doris, who would have been tickled to know that her own clever hand-making skills played such a large part in leading me to this moment.

# PHOTO AND ILLUSTRATION CREDITS

THE FOLLOWING IMAGES COURTESY OF
THE NEW YORK PUBLIC LIBRARY, ASTOR,
LENOX, AND TILDEN FOUNDATIONS:

Pages 13 & 145: *Godey's Lady's Book*,
November 1849. Mid-Manhattan Picture
Collection.

Pages 15, 118, 122 & 125: Selected pages
from *Photographs of British Algae: Cyanotype
Impressions* by Anna Atkins. [Halstead Place,
Sevenoaks, England: Anna Atkins, 1843-
1853.] Spencer Collection.

Page 21: *Combinaisons Ornementales se
Multipliant à l'Infini à l'Aide du Miroir.
Paris: Librairie Centrale* des Beaux-Arts,
[1900?]: The Miriam and Ira D. Wallach
Division of Art, Prints and Photographs:
Art & Architecture Collection. Stag's Head,
*Godey's Lady's Book* (August 1867) and
*Shawl, Peterson's Magazine* (May 1862): Mid-
Manhattan Picture Collection. *The Mordant
Dyestuffs of the Farbenfabriken vorm. Friedr.
Bayer Co., Elberfeld...* New York, 1902: SIBL
General Collection.

Page 24: *Kokushi Daijiten.* Tokyo: Yoshikawa
Kobunkan, [1908.] General Research Division.

Page 68: Endpapers from Voltaire's *La Pucelle
d'Orleans.* Manuscript, [175-?.] Martin J.
Gross Collection, Rare Book Division.

Page 76 & 78: Horace Grant Healey
Penmanship Collection. Manuscripts &
Archives Division.

Page 81: Page from John Seddon's *The
Pen-Mans Paradis...* London: Wm. Court,
[1695.] Detail from George Bickham's *The
Universal Penman.* London, 1733-41. Rare
Book Division.

Page 89: *Specimen of Leavenworth's Patent
Wood Type, Manufactured by J.M. Debow.*
[Allentown, N.J., 184-?.] Rare Book Division.

Page 90: *Prue & I* by George William Curtis,
1892, in Club Bindery binding. Spencer
Collection.

Page 108: Selected page from *Factorum et
Dictorum Memorabilium Libri X* by Valerius
Maximus. Spencer Collection.

Pages 2 & 110: Illustrations by Jessie Willcox
Smith in Johanna Spyri's *Heidi.* Philadelphia:
David McKay Co., 1922. General Research
Division.

Page 117: Illustration by Willebeek Le Mair
from *Children's Corner.* Philadelphia: McKay,
1915. Mid-Manhattan Picture Collection.

Pages 141 & 142: Selected pages from Pierre
Joseph Redouté's *Les Roses.* Paris: Didot,
1817 [-1824.] Spencer Collection.

Page 146: *Godey's Magazine* poster by
Carlton C. Fowler (June 1896.) The Miriam
and Ira D. Wallach Division of Art, Prints and
Photographs: Art & Architecture Collection.

Page 149: Dogwood from François André
Michaux's *The North American Sylva; or, A
Description of the Forest Trees...* Philadelphia:
J. Dobson, Printed by William Amphlett, New
Harmony, Ind., 1841-49. General Research
Division.

Page 151: Illustration from *Pictorial Review*
(January 1916.) Mid-Manhattan Picture
Collection.

Page 152: Detail from Herman Moll's *New
and exact map of the dominions of the King
of Great Britain on ye continent of North
America.* [1736?] The Lionel Pincus and
Princess Firyal Map Division.

Page 157: Virginia, Marylandia et Carolina
in America septentrionali Britannorum
industria excultae / repraesentatae à Ioh.
Bapt. Homann, S.C.M. Geog. [1714-1730?]
The Lionel Pincus and Princess Firyal Map
Division.

Page 158: Battista Agnese's land map of
Cyprus in portolan atlas. [ca. 1552.] Spencer
Collection.

Page 181: Chesterfield House from Isaac
Ware's *A Complete Body of Architecture:
Adorned with Plans and Elevations.* London:
T. Osborne and J. Shipton, 1756. The Miriam
and Ira D. Wallach Division of Art, Prints and
Photographs: Art & Architecture Collection.

Page 190: Heart-shaped leaves design from
Henri Gillet's *Nouvelles Fantasies Decoratives:
36 Compositions en Couleur.* Paris: Ch.
Massin, [ca. 1880–1920.] The Miriam and
Ira D. Wallach Division of Art, Prints and
Photographs: Art & Architecture Collection.

ADDITIONAL CREDITS:
Pages 67 (marbled paper) and 189 (*Mrs.
Owens' Cook Book and Useful Household
Hints,* Chicago: J.B. Smiley, 1892): images
provided by author.

Page 121: "Luna Moth" from *Field Folly
Snow: Poems* by Cecily Parks. Copyright 2008
by Cecily Parks. Used with permission of
University of Georgia Press.

Pages 126 & 131: Selected woodcuts from
Conrad Gessner's *Historia Animalium.* Tiguri:
Apud Christ. Froschouerum, 1551–1558.
Courtesy of Historical Anatomies on the
Web, National Library of Medicine (NLM,)
Bethesda, Maryland.

Page 140: "Coming Attractions," *American
Hairdresser,* January 1948. Courtesy of
*American Salon Magazine.*

Page 163: Edmond Doran's *Portolan Chart
of Mediterranean.* 1586. Courtesy of General
Collection, Beinecke Rare Book and
Manuscript Library, Yale University.

Page 194: Hubert Morley's "Your Victory
Garden Counts More Than Ever!"
Government Printing Office, 1945. Courtesy
of Illinois Digital Archives (IDA) and Illinois
State Library.

PROP CREDITS:
Page 77: Cookies from One Girl Cookie; mugs
from Fishs Eddy

Page 133: Stool from Sundance Catalog

Page 165: Glassware from Fishs Eddy

Note: *Italic* page numbers indicate photographs.

# ABOUT THE AUTHOR

*Jessica Pigza is a rare book librarian who knits and stitches in her spare time. She is currently the assistant curator of the New York Public Library's Rare Book Division. She shares her Brooklyn apartment with her husband, her dog, and her own growing library of vintage craft books. Visit her website at www.handmadelibrarian.com.*

PUBLISHED IN 2014 BY STEWART, TABORI & CHANG
AN IMPRINT OF ABRAMS

LIBRARY OF CONGRESS CONTROL
NUMBER: 2013945655
ISBN: 978-1-61769-096-9

EDITOR: MELANIE FALICK
DESIGNER: DEB WOOD
PRODUCTION MANAGER: TINA CAMERON

PRINTED AND BOUND IN CHINA
10 9 8 7 6 5 4 3 2 1

THE ART OF BOOKS SINCE 1949
115 WEST 18TH STREET
NEW YORK, NY 10011
WWW.ABRAMSBOOKS.COM